CAMPAIGN • 237

THE FOURTH CRUSADE 1202–04

The betrayal of Byzantium

DAVID NICOLLE   ILLUSTRATED BY CHRISTA HOOK

Series editor Marcus Cowper

First published in 2011 by Osprey Publishing
Midland House, West Way, Botley, Oxford OX2 0PH, UK
44-02 23rd St, Suite 219, Long Island City, NY 11101, USA

E-mail: info@ospreypublishing.com

OSPREY PUBLISHING IS PART OF THE OSPREY GROUP

ISBN: 978 1 84908 319 5

E-book ISBN: 978 1 84908 320 1

Editorial by Ilios Publishing Ltd, Oxford, UK (www.iliospublishing.com)
Design: The Black Spot
Index by Marie-Pierre Evans
Originated by PDQ Media
Cartography: Bounford.com
Bird's-eye view artworks: The Black Spot
Printed in China through World Print Ltd.

11 12 13 14 15   10 9 8 7 6 5 4 3 2 1

www.ospreypublishing.com

DEDICATION

For the Reverend Rolf Hjorth, a full life lived to the full.

ARTIST'S NOTE

Readers may care to note that the original paintings from which the colour plates in this book were prepared are available for private sale. The Publishers retain all reproduction copyright whatsoever. All enquiries should be addressed to:

Scorpio Gallery,
PO Box 475,
Hailsham,
East Sussex BN27 2SL
United Kingdom

The Publishers regret that they can enter into no correspondence upon this matter.

THE WOODLAND TRUST

Osprey Publishing are supporting the Woodland Trust, the UK's leading woodland conservation charity, by funding the dedication of trees.

Key to military symbols

XXXXX	XXXX	XXX	XX	X	III	II
Army Group	Army	Corps	Division	Brigade	Regiment	Battalion

Company/Battery	Infantry	Artillery	Cavalry

Key to unit identification

Unit identifier — Parent unit
Commander
(+) with added elements
(−) less elements

CONTENTS

4

ORIGINS OF THE CAMPAIGN

If the crusades have become controversial, the Fourth Crusade always was so. Until modern times the idea of Christians and Muslims slaughtering each other in the name of religion seemed almost acceptable, but the idea of Latin Catholic Crusaders turning against fellow Christians of the Orthodox Church shocked many people, even at the time, and came to be described as 'The Great Betrayal'. It was even blamed for so undermining the Greek-speaking Byzantine state that this relic of the ancient Roman Empire succumbed to the Ottoman Turks. In reality the Fourth Crusade was not that straightforward; nor was its aftermath inevitable.

The Fourth Crusade was a consequence of the deeply disappointing though gratifyingly heroic Third Crusade, which had failed to regain the Holy City of Jerusalem from Saladin. On 8 January 1198 a new pope, the hugely ambitious Innocent III, took the reins of power in Rome. In August he proclaimed a new crusade, the declared purpose of which was to liberate Jerusalem from the 'infidel' by invading Egypt, the chief centre of Muslim power in the eastern Mediterranean. It was also the most important sultanate in the Ayyubid Empire founded by Saladin. Those who dreamed of destroying

OPPOSITE
Byzantine wall painting of a warrior saint made in the late 12th or early 13th century, in the monastery church of Panagia Kosmosotira, Feres, on the frontier between Greece and Turkey. (Author's photograph)

RIGHT
Carved ivory panel showing allegorical figures of Peace and War, Byzantine, 11th–12th century. (Hermitage Museum, St Petersburg. Author's photograph)

Europe and the Middle East, *c.*1195

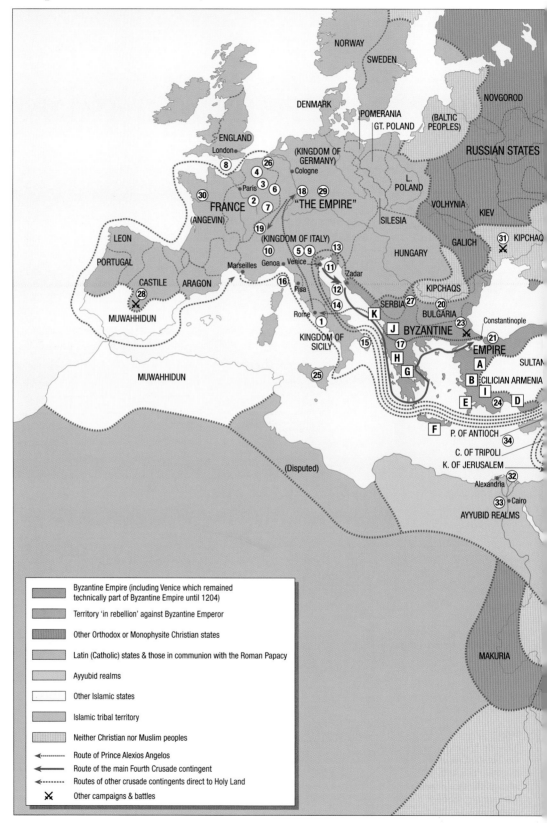

Legend:

- Byzantine Empire (including Venice which remained technically part of Byzantine Empire until 1204)
- Territory 'in rebellion' against Byzantine Emperor
- Other Orthodox or Monophysite Christian states
- Latin (Catholic) states & those in communion with the Roman Papacy
- Ayyubid realms
- Other Islamic states
- Islamic tribal territory
- Neither Christian nor Muslim peoples
- ········→ Route of Prince Alexios Angelos
- ───→ Route of the main Fourth Crusade contingent
- ┄┄→ Routes of other crusade contingents direct to Holy Land
- ✕ Other campaigns & battles

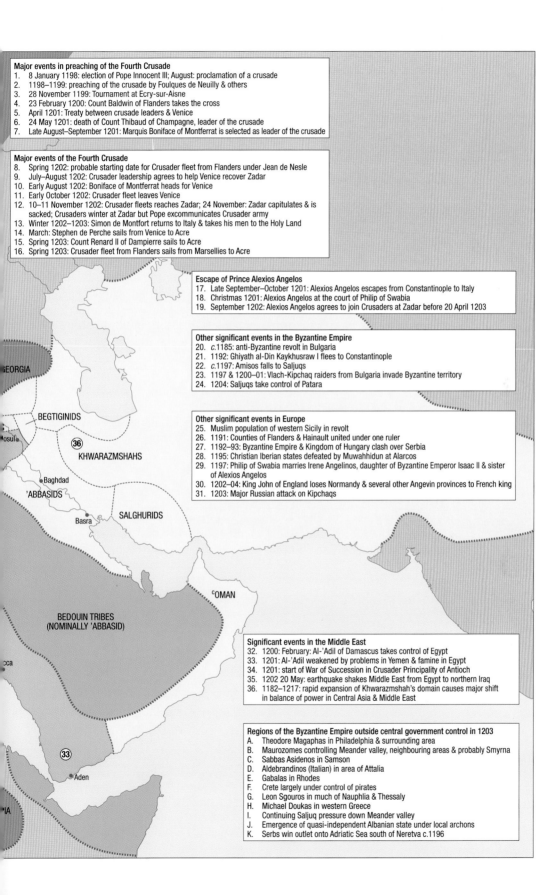

Major events in preaching of the Fourth Crusade
1. 8 January 1198: election of Pope Innocent III; August: proclamation of a crusade
2. 1198–1199: preaching of the crusade by Foulques de Neuilly & others
3. 28 November 1199: Tournament at Ecry-sur-Aisne
4. 23 February 1200: Count Baldwin of Flanders takes the cross
5. April 1201: Treaty between crusade leaders & Venice
6. 24 May 1201: death of Count Thibaud of Champagne, leader of the crusade
7. Late August–September 1201: Marquis Boniface of Montferrat is selected as leader of the crusade

Major events of the Fourth Crusade
8. Spring 1202: probable starting date for Crusader fleet from Flanders under Jean de Nesle
9. July–August 1202: Crusader leadership agrees to help Venice recover Zadar
10. Early August 1202: Boniface of Montferrat heads for Venice
11. Early October 1202: Crusader fleet leaves Venice
12. 10–11 November 1202: Crusader fleets reaches Zadar; 24 November: Zadar capitulates & is sacked; Crusaders winter at Zadar but Pope excommunicates Crusader army
13. Winter 1202–1203: Simon de Montfort returns to Italy & takes his men to the Holy Land
14. March: Stephen de Perche sails from Venice to Acre
15. Spring 1203: Count Renard II of Dampierre sails to Acre
16. Spring 1203: Crusader fleet from Flanders sails from Marsellies to Acre

Escape of Prince Alexios Angelos
17. Late September–October 1201: Alexios Angelos escapes from Constantinople to Italy
18. Christmas 1201: Alexios Angelos at the court of Philip of Swabia
19. September 1202: Alexios Angelos agrees to join Crusaders at Zadar before 20 April 1203

Other significant events in the Byzantine Empire
20. c.1185: anti-Byzantine revolt in Bulgaria
21. 1192: Ghiyath al-Din Kaykhusraw I flees to Constantinople
22. c.1197: Amisos falls to Saljuqs
23. 1197 & 1200–01: Vlach-Kipchaq raiders from Bulgaria invade Byzantine territory
24. 1204: Saljuqs take control of Patara

Other significant events in Europe
25. Muslim population of western Sicily in revolt
26. 1191: Counties of Flanders & Hainault united under one ruler
27. 1192–93: Byzantine Empire & Kingdom of Hungary clash over Serbia
28. 1195: Christian Iberian states defeated by Muwahhidun at Alarcos
29. 1197: Philip of Swabia marries Irene Angelinos, daughter of Byzantine Emperor Isaac II & sister of Alexios Angelos
30. 1202–04: King John of England loses Normandy & several other Angevin provinces to French king
31. 1203: Major Russian attack on Kipchaqs

Significant events in the Middle East
32. 1200: February: Al-'Adil of Damascus takes control of Egypt
33. 1201: Al-'Adil weakened by problems in Yemen & famine in Egypt
34. 1201: start of War of Succession in Crusader Principality of Antioch
35. 1202 20 May: earthquake shakes Middle East from Egypt to northern Iraq
36. 1182–1217: rapid expansion of Khwarazmshah's domain causes major shift in balance of power in Central Asia & Middle East

Regions of the Byzantine Empire outside central government control in 1203
A. Theodore Magaphas in Philadelphia & surrounding area
B. Maurozomes controlling Meander valley, neighbouring areas & probably Smyrna
C. Sabbas Asidenos in Samson
D. Aldebrandinos (Italian) in area of Attalia
E. Gabalas in Rhodes
F. Crete largely under control of pirates
G. Leon Sgouros in much of Nauphlia & Thessaly
H. Michael Doukas in western Greece
I. Continuing Saljuq pressure down Meander valley
J. Emergence of quasi-independent Albanian state under local archons
K. Serbs win outlet onto Adriatic Sea south of Neretva c.1196

GEORGIA

BEGTIGINIDS

Mosul

KHWARAZMSHAHS

Baghdad

'ABBASIDS

Basra

SALGHURIDS

cOMAN

BEDOUIN TRIBES
(NOMINALLY 'ABBASID)

cca

Aden

IA

the Islamic Middle East had now recognized that Egypt was the key, but if their strategy was correct then their planning was not. The realities of power, money, climate and the availability of food to sustain a crusading army would cause the greater part of the Fourth Crusade to be diverted against fellow Christians. Its first victim would be the largely Latin city of Zadar (then called Zara); the second would be Constantinople, capital of the Byzantine Empire and the biggest, wealthiest and most cultured city in Christendom.

BYZANTIUM AND ITS NEIGHBOURS

Relations between the Orthodox Byzantine Empire and its Latin neighbours had been close but complex for centuries. However, the differences that seem obvious today were not necessarily seen that way at the time. Nor was the Byzantine Empire necessarily a declining power in need of Western help. Under the 12th-century Comnenid dynasty Byzantium appeared a powerful state bent on regaining territory from its Muslim eastern neighbours and from its Christian neighbours in the Balkans, Italy and even central Europe. Meanwhile, in Western Europe a remarkable economic revolution had already started more than a century earlier, yet it was still somewhat backward, warlike and aggressive. One area where Western superiority was already established was at sea, most of the Mediterranean now being dominated by Italian sailors and merchants. Amalfi had been first on the scene and its people had their own distinct quarter in Constantinople, where the Greeks regarded these Amalfitans as being almost as civilized as themselves. Following close behind, and already more powerful than Amalfi, were the merchant republics of Pisa, Genoa and Venice. The former two had a reputation for ferocity, often directed against each other, while the Venetians were theoretically still subjects of the Byzantine Empire, and would remain so until 1204.

Most crusades to the Middle East already relied upon naval power. However, the Fourth Crusade was an entirely maritime expedition, which cannot be understood without some appreciation of early 13th-century

A flanking tower of the Burj al-Gharbi ('Western Gate') in Alexandria, which was the original target of the Fourth Crusade. (Author's photograph)

Mediterranean nautical knowledge. This was more advanced than is generally realized, the sailors possessing geographical knowledge that would not be written down for centuries. For example, there is strong evidence that simple forms of *portolano* coastal maps were used at a time when the famous medieval *mappe mundi* made by monks offered fanciful and entirely useless images of the known world. It is thus highly unlikely that popes and other rulers failed to use such information when planning major military expeditions overseas. On the other hand the merchants, sailors and governments involved in supposedly illegal trade with Islamic powers preferred to remain discreet.

In contrast there was an extraordinary amount of misinformation in Western Europe that exaggerated, though did not entirely invent, the friendly relations between later 12th-century Byzantine emperors and Saladin or his successors. To this were added lurid stories about the supposed weakness, effeminacy and corruption of the 'Greeks', which reflected the undoubtedly sophisticated and often unwarlike character of the Byzantine ruling elite.

Alongside these negative images of Byzantium there was a dream of Latin–Byzantine cooperation against the 'infidel', which had existed for centuries. The ideal appeared in a later 12th-century version in *chansons de geste* epic poems such as *Girart de Roussillon*, although here Constantinople is a distant and strange place. Another manifestation is found in the 13th-century *Chanson du Pèlerinage de Charlemagne*, which was probably based upon a lost 12th-century or late 11th-century original. Constantinople is again portrayed as an almost magical city, perhaps reflecting fear of Byzantine technology and science.

A period of relative peace and stability had followed Saladin's death in 1193, with both the rump Kingdom of Jerusalem and Saladin's Ayyubid successors seemingly convinced that little was to be gained from further warfare. Early in 1200, however, the political and military situation changed dramatically when Saladin's younger brother al-'Adil Sayf al-Din ('Saphadin' to the Crusaders), who already ruled Damascus, Jerusalem and parts of the Jazira (Mesopotamia), also took control of Egypt. As a result he was generally, if not universally, recognized as head of the 'Ayyubid Empire'. Al-'Adil's position was confirmed when, two years later, he was also recognized as overlord in Aleppo. For the first time in nine years Saladin's realm was reunited and again virtually surrounded what remained of the Crusader states.

A lance-armed cavalryman pursuing a horse archer was a popular motif in Byzantine art, these being on an engraved late 12th- or early 13th-century bronze bowl. (Hermitage Museum, St Petersburg)

9

Another significant player in this region was the Saljuq Turkish Sultanate of Rum (Rome), which was how Arabs, Turks and Persians knew the 'Late Roman' or Byzantine Empire. Unfortunately there is still a great deal of uncertainty about quite where the frontier zone lay between the Byzantine Empire and the Saljuq Sultanate of Rum around the time of the Fourth Crusade. For example, Lycia in south-western Anatolia had been a sort of no man's land since the late 11th century. Meanwhile, the Saljuq Sultanate itself was going through a period of profound cultural, economic and military change, with many Saljuq Turkish cities being characterized by a thriving multicultural civilization incorporating Turkish, Greek and Armenian, Muslim and Christian elements. The overall impression of cultural coexistence also undermines the clarity of a supposed cultural frontier between Byzantium and the Turks.

Political tensions within the Saljuq Sultanate of Rum resulted from Sultan Qilij Arslan II dividing his realm into *iqtas* (fiefs) for his eight sons in accordance with Saljuq tradition. After his death in 1192, the Sultanate suffered from a long civil war caused by Rukn al-Din Sulayman II Ibn Qilij Arslan stripping his brothers of their domains. One of the latter was Ghiyath al-Din Kaykhusraw, who took refuge in Constantinople where he married a woman from a powerful Byzantine family.

The situation was similarly complex in Europe where, for example, rivalry between the Italian maritime republics had been fierce for centuries. Yet any successful crusade to the Middle East would depend upon support from at least one of them. Furthermore, their rivalry concerned their relationships with the Byzantine Empire. Genoa and Pisa were often at war during this period, but Byzantium gave trading privileges to both in an attempt to avoid a Venetian preponderance in Byzantine trade. The Fourth Crusade would, in fact, see Pisan and Genoese residents of Constantinople fighting alongside their Byzantine neighbours in defence of the city against Venetians and Crusaders.

Another significant power within Italy was, of course, the papacy itself. Pope Innocent III has been described as one of the great figures in papal history. He was certainly one of the most ambitious popes, though in the end his wide-ranging plans often came to nothing or even proved counter-productive. Innocent III's dream of a great new crusade certainly backfired.

Foulques de Neuilly was given a leading role in preaching this new expedition in 1198 and 1199. Unfortunately, Foulques was so obsessed with 'moral rectitude' that he offended several of the rulers and powerful aristocrats who were needed as potential leaders, including King Richard I of England. Furthermore, Foulques' lack of tact undermined his attempt to reconcile the bickering (but militarily important) kingdoms of England and France. The impossibility of papal control over its own preachers of crusade certainly led to confusion. Whether this contributed to a lack of focus in the eventual expedition is impossible to say.

VENICE AND THE CRUSADERS

One state eventually dominated the story of the Fourth Crusade: the Republic of Venice. Until 1204 Venice remained theoretically part of the Byzantine Empire, though in practical terms its elected duke, or 'doge', was by now an independent ruler. On the other hand, a close and ancient association with Constantinople gave Venice huge commercial advantages over its rivals – to some extent even over the indigenous merchants of the Byzantine Empire. Lying along the vital Venetian trade route down the Adriatic Sea lay the rugged coast and multiple islands of Dalmatia, where a largely Italianized population had dominated towns and some stretches of coast since Roman times. For most of the early medieval period Dalmatia was dominated by the Byzantine Empire, often through its proxy, the Doge of Venice, as 'Dux Dalmatie'. In practical terms this could result in Dalmatian towns promising fidelity to Venice in return for Venetian protection, while at the same time remaining effectively autonomous.

During the 12th century however, the joint Kingdom of Hungary and Croatia dominated much of Dalmatia. This the Venetians saw as a threat to their trade routes, and as a result two port-cities, Zadar (Zara) and Split

Medieval Venetian art was under very strong Byzantine influence, as seen in the costume and weaponry shown on this 12th-century Venetian ivory panel. (Victoria and Albert Museum, inv. 295-1867, London)

The gilded interior of St Mark's Cathedral in Venice mirrored that of the Hagia Sophia in Constantinople. (Author's photograph)

(Spalato), became the focal points in a bitter rivalry; Venice generally dominated the former while Hungary dominated the latter. A short-lived Byzantine revival under the Comnenid emperors pushed back the Hungarians in the 1160s and 1170s, but Byzantine authority then collapsed again, leaving Venice to face a dangerous situation.

Elsewhere in Europe, internal problems or hostility between major states meant that no king or emperor was available to take command of the new crusade. There had, for example, been a notable deterioration in relations between the Byzantine and Holy Roman Empires during the second half of the 12th century. The former was the direct heir of the eastern half of the ancient Roman Empire, while the latter claimed to be heir to the western half, as revived by Charlemagne in the 8th century. Nevertheless, the ruling dynasties of the Holy Roman and Byzantine Empires did forge dynastic links, which, though they achieved little, had an influence upon the course of the Fourth Crusade.

The situation in France and England was even less encouraging for Pope Innocent III's new crusade. King Richard of England died in 1199 and his brother, King John, inherited his quarrel with King Philip Augustus of France. As a result of this, official French and English participation in the expedition was impossible, though large numbers of French, Anglo-French and Anglo-Norman knights did take the cross. In fact the year 1204, when the Byzantine capital fell under Crusader control, was also a very significant year in French and English history – Philip Augustus expelling his Anglo-Angevin rivals from all of France except for Gascony in the far south-west and the Channel Islands in the far north-west.

Another area that would play a major role in the forthcoming crusade, and its leadership, was Flanders. Though a feudal fiefdom of the Kingdom of France rather than an independent state, Flanders had become an important, wealthy and strongly urbanized part of Western Europe. During the decade before the Fourth Crusade the Count of Flanders' power had declined and, despite being economically very developed, the area remained politically somewhat anarchic. The situation was further complicated by the neighbouring counties of Flanders and Hainault having being ruled by one person since 1191, despite Flanders being within the Kingdom of France and Hainault being part of the German Empire.

Dalmatia was part of Croatia, which had been a joint kingdom with Hungary since 1102, and became the first victim of the Fourth Crusade despite the fact that King Imre of Hungary and Croatia had himself taken the cross. Much of Dalmatia was nevertheless outside any government's control. Here the Latin aristocracy of the coastal cities despised the surrounding Slav peasantry and tribesmen. Each of the old Roman cities also retained their autonomy and frequently competed with each other, while loyalties were very localized, much as they were in Italy.

Meanwhile, the relationship between Catholic Hungary and Orthodox Byzantium had long been close, though not always friendly. During the first half of the 12th century these two huge realms had been allies, after which Hungary found itself resisting Byzantine expansion until a sudden collapse of Byzantine power in the later 12th century. It was during these years that Hungary seized extensive territory in ex-Byzantine Serbia and regained much of Dalmatia, where it found itself in competition with Venice. The glorious reign of King Béla III ended in 1196, being followed by that of Béla's son Imre (1196–1204), which saw civil war between the king and his younger brother Andrew. Meanwhile the pope urged Imre to lead a crusade against Bogomil heretics who had established themselves in Bosnia and various other parts of the Balkans.

The sudden decline of Byzantine imperial power in the later 12th century permitted the re-emergence of independent or autonomous entities across much of the Balkans. The first Albanian state emerged around 1190 under its own 'archons', or local leaders; this independence then being lost to the Byzantine Despotate of Epirus in 1216. In most of the Balkan Peninsula Orthodox Christianity provided a regional identity but no real unity, while this separateness from their western and northern neighbours was also reinforced by the Balkan peoples' essentially Byzantine cultural heritage.

Like Albania, Bosnia and Serbia emerged as separate entities. However, much of what would later be the southern part of medieval Serbia initially exchanged Byzantine for Bulgarian domination. Furthermore, as Byzantine authority declined, so Hungarian pressure continued and a Hungarian army actually reached Sofia in the late 1180s. Indeed, competition between Byzantium and Hungary for domination over the lower-Danube region remained a feature of this period.

The outbreak of a revolt in what is now Bulgaria in the mid-1180s then forced the Byzantines back to the Danube Delta on the Black Sea coast. Credit for initiating and leading this revolt, which resulted in the establishment of the 'Second Bulgarian Empire', remains a source of heated nationalistic debate between Bulgarians and Romanians, three peoples actually being involved: Romanian-speaking Vlachs, Turkish-speaking Kipchaqs (Cumans) and Slav-speaking Bulgarians. By the time of the Fourth Crusade a Byzantine counter-attack had faltered and the new state had emerged in the northern part of what is now Bulgaria, while Byzantine authority was restricted to the lowlands of eastern Thrace. In 1201 or 1202, as the Crusaders were mustering in the west, the Vlachs and Kipchaqs again raided Byzantine territory, getting dangerously close to Constantinople. This was followed by a peace agreement between the Byzantine Emperor Alexios III and Bulgarian King Ivan II, otherwise known as Ioannitsa or as 'Kaloyan the Romanslayer'. This remained the situation when the Fourth Crusade suddenly appeared on the scene in 1203.

The preliminary sketch for a Byzantine wall painting, made some time after 1171, from the church at Durdevi Stupovi near Novi Pazar. (National Museum, Belgrade. Author's photograph)

The Byzantine Empire has naturally been the subject of intense historical research to discover quite how and why a once-mighty (and still extensive) state with its massively fortified and hugely wealthy capital fell so suddenly to a handful of crusading adventurers and their Venetian allies. No simple answer has been agreed, because there is no simple answer. The weaknesses of Byzantium at the time of the Fourth Crusade were manifold, though none of them fully accounts for this collapse. On the other hand there are a number of basic facts. During the 12th century the Byzantine Empire made significant territorial gains in the Balkans and this is believed to have resulted in a shift of emphasis from the Anatolian or Asian provinces to the European provinces. Nevertheless, it is far from clear how important the regions north of the Rhodope Mountains were, either economically, politically or militarily.

Similarly, Emperor Manuel's massive defeat at the hands of the Saljuq Turks at the battle of Myriokephalon in 1176 may not have been as important as once thought. Certainly the Saljuqs chose not to follow up their success by conquering additional Byzantine territory. Similarly, the Byzantine army continued to defend the empire's frontiers with reasonable success until its collapse in the late 12th and early 13th centuries.

Tensions between the indigenous, largely Greek, population of the empire and the Latin, largely Italian, merchant communities in the major cities also seem exaggerated. In fact the Byzantine populace turned against these economically dominant foreigners only when the latter got drawn into Byzantine political rivalries. Then, of course, there were appalling massacres such as that of 1182. Michael Angold, the renowned historian of this period, summarized the situation immediately prior to 1204 as follows: 'Ever since the death of Manuel I Komnenos in 1180 the weaknesses of the Byzantine Empire had become increasingly apparent. By the end of the century there was an atmosphere of complete demoralization. There was vicious intrigue and corruption in the capital, anarchy in the provinces, and growing external pressure on the boundaries of the empire'.[1] However, the Fourth Crusade was more than merely another element in this disintegration, instead it converted a threatening situation into a complete catastrophe.

CONSTANTINOPLE'S HOLLOW EMPIRE

Hindsight is probably more dangerous when studying the Fourth Crusade than any other crusade. Few if any people at the time realized quite how hollow a shell Byzantium had become. To its citizens, the Byzantine Empire was still the Roman Empire; it was Romania to most Westerners and Rum to most Muslims. Its people, its rulers and presumably most of its soldiers retained a massive sense of cultural, administrative and military superiority. A dip in this confidence had followed the catastrophic battle of Manzikert in

1 Angold, M., A Byzantine Government in Exile (Oxford, 1975) p. 9.

1071, with some cultural or religious leaders criticizing the empire's concern with self-enrichment and pleasure, but this proved to be a passing phase and the self-satisfied Byzantine self-image had been restored by 1203. Byzantine pride in the empire and its capital apparently meant that the people envisaged heaven as an improved, purified and infinitely successful version of their own state. Certainly the majority believed that their state was under the special protection of God, Christ and his saints.

The city of Constantinople was far larger and more sophisticated than any other in Christendom. Several estimates of its population have been suggested, though a figure of around 500,000 seems most likely. Foreign visitors were also clearly impressed. One such was the Jewish scholar and traveller Benjamin of Tudela in northern Spain, who wrote: 'Constantinople is a busy city, and merchants come to it from every country by sea or land, and there is none like it in the world except Baghdad, the great city of Islam... A quantity of wealth beyond telling is brought hither year by year.' Benjamin also described the imperial Blachernae Palace: 'He [the Emperor] overlaid its columns and walls with gold and silver, and engraved thereon representations of the battles before his day and of his own combats. He also set up a throne of gold and precious stones, and a golden crown was suspended by a golden chain over the throne, so arranged that he might sit thereunder.'[2]

A more than usually realistic illustration of a soldier in a 12th-century Byzantine manuscript. (*Works of John Chrysostom*, Bibliothèque Nationale, Ms. Gr. 806, f.94v, Paris)

Much was made of a supposed Byzantine economic collapse in the later 12th century; however, some recent historians have disputed this interpretation, even suggesting that the economy was expanding until stopped by the catastrophic Fourth Crusade. What is certain is that Constantinople itself was hugely wealthy in 1203. It is also worth noting that the city's population was apparently fed with grain from Thrace, Macedonia and Thessaly, most of which were still under imperial control.

For an empire in which religion was a central aspect of identity it seems odd that the Orthodox Church had actually become a source of weakness. By the time of the Fourth Crusade it was wracked by doctrinal disagreements and bitterly competing factions. Nevertheless, most of its leaders and adherents remained passionately opposed to the pope's equally insistent claims to the leadership of the entire Christian world. Written exchanges between the Patriarch of Constantinople, John X Camaterus, and Pope Innocent III were as fierce as ever on the eve of the Fourth Crusade, yet within the Byzantine Empire there was no apparent fear of the Orthodox Church being militarily conquered by a Latin Catholic army.

Nor was Byzantine society unified religiously or linguistically. For centuries the Emperors had forcibly resettled defeated invaders or rebels in different parts of their empire. The largest groups were Slav or Turkish, and although such resettled communities were assimilated into local populations, this process took time. Another group retained a separate identity until the end; the Armenians not only spoke a different language but adhered to a

2 Adler, M. N. (tr.), *The Itinerary of Benjamin of Tudela* (Malibu, 1987) pp. 70–71.

different branch of Christianity. Their importance and numbers within the Byzantine administration and army had declined during the 12th century, but one substantial community lived in north-western Anatolia, around Abydos (Nara Burnu). Even here, far from their ancestral homeland in eastern Anatolia, the Armenians resisted Hellenization and were in turn deeply mistrusted by the Greeks. Their fate in the immediate aftermath of the Fourth Crusade would be a tragic one.

The Byzantines have often been portrayed as both fearing and despising outsiders, yet this has again probably been exaggerated. For example, Byzantine 'lives of the saints' dating from the 12th century often expressed a positive view of the Latin Catholic West, especially of Italy and the papal city of Rome. Nor were Westerners regarded as much of a threat. Even the aggressive Normans of southern Italy, who had so often invaded Byzantine territory, had recently been defeated. Indeed, Emperor Manuel Comnenus admired Western military systems and some other aspects of Western European civilization. Less known is the fact that Manuel also admired Turkish things, and had a chamber in his palace decorated in Turkish style. Of course Byzantine respect for Muslim Arab and Persian civilization went back much further.

Byzantine Greeks may have had a huge sense of cultural superiority but they were rarely xenophobic, despite the multitude of external threats to their empire. The last major Siculo-Norman invasion had been crushed in 1185, but the victorious Byzantine general Alexios Branas then revolted against the emperor, eventually being defeated and killed by Conrad of Montferrat. The latter was an Italian nobleman who had recently married Emperor Isaac's sister, Theodora, and would briefly be the nominal King of Jerusalem. As a result the name Montferrat was long remembered in Constantinople, which was of some significance when Conrad's brother Boniface of Montferrat appeared before the city walls as nominal leader of the Fourth Crusade.

The Saljuq Turkish threat seemingly revived in the later 12th century, when authority within Byzantine Anatolia was seriously weakened. However, the fragmentation of the empire was probably a greater problem before the Fourth Crusade. Within the Anatolian provinces alone a nobleman named Theodore Magaphas had installed himself in Philadelphia (Ala ehir) and soon controlled a wide area; another man named Maurozomes dominated the Meander Valley and neighbouring areas, perhaps including Smyrna (Izmir), while the Comnenid family dominated the region around Trebizond (Trabzon). Some of these autonomous governors also used Turkish help to maintain themselves.

The situation had reached such a point in 1204 that the leaders of the Fourth Crusade, when they agreed the *Partitio Romaniae*, which would divide the Byzantine Empire once it had been conquered, left regions like Smyrna, Trebizond, Rhodes and most other Aegean islands out of their calculations. Perhaps this was because these areas were no longer dominated by the Byzantine Emperor in Constantinople at that time. Whether the Crusaders similarly gave up on those European provinces that were currently out of central-government control is less clear. This, then, was the ramshackle Byzantine Empire as the Crusaders gathered in Venice.

CHRONOLOGY

1198

8 January	Election of Pope Innocent III.
August	Proclamation of a crusade.

1198–99

Preaching of the crusade by Foulques de Neuilly.

1199

28 November	Tournament at Ecry-sur-Aisne, where the Counts of Champagne and Blois take the cross.

1200

February	Al-'Adil, the Ayyubid ruler of Damascus, Jerusalem and parts of the Jazira takes control of Egypt and is recognized as leader of the Ayyubid Empire.
23 February	Count Baldwin of Flanders takes the cross.

1201

Throughout year	Sultan al-'Adil is weakened by problems in Yemen and ongoing famine in Egypt.
April	Treaty between crusade leaders and Venice to transport 4,500 horsemen to the Holy Land.
24 May	Death of the nominated leader of the crusade, Count Thibaud of Champagne.
Summer	Marquis Boniface of Montferrat takes the cross and is selected as leader of the crusade; Church discussion at Cîteaux; many Burgundians take the cross.
Late September to October	Prince Alexios Angelos escapes from Constantinople and heads for Italy but is rebuffed by the pope.
Around Christmas	Prince Alexios Angelos at the court of Philip of Swabia, King of Germany, seeking support, and meets Boniface of Montferrat.

1202

March	Al-'Adil gains suzerainty over Aleppo, confirming his position as leader of the Ayyubid Empire.
April–May	Most Crusaders head for Venice.
20 May	Major earthquake shakes the Middle East from Egypt to northern Iraq, causing severe damage in Palestine, Lebanon and western Syria, including the fortification of the main Crusader city of Acre.
29 June	Original date planned for the departure of the Crusader fleet, nothing happens.

July–August	The Crusader leadership cannot pay Venice for the fleet; they agree to help Venice recover Zadar.	16 May	Forces of Crusader Principality of Tripoli defeated by those of the Muslim governor of Ba'albak near Ba'rin.
8 September	Doge Enrico Dandolo takes the cross.	24 May	Crusader fleet leaves Corfu.
September	Emissaries from Prince Alexios Angelos win support from crusade leaders; Alexios agrees to join the crusade army at Zadar before 20 April 1203.	May–June	Main Crusader fleet rounds Greece; several smaller Crusader contingents arrive in Acre (May to August); a current truce between the Crusader Kingdom of Jerusalem and the Ayyubid ruler of Egypt and Damascus leads to arguments because the Crusaders want to attack the Muslims immediately.
Early October	Crusader fleet leaves Venice in two divisions.		
10–11 November	Crusader fleets reaches Zadar, which it besieges.	3 June	The Muslim ruler of Hims defeats the Hospitallers and Principality of Tripoli; Templars unsuccessfully attempt to negotiate a truce on behalf of the Hospitallers.
24 November	Zadar capitulates and is sacked.		
November 1202 to April 1203	Pope Innocent III excommunicates the Crusader army, which winters at Zadar; many Crusaders leave the army.	23 June	Crusader fleet arrives before Constantinople (Istanbul).

1203

January	Agreement between Crusader negotiators and Prince Alexios to help him become the Byzantine Emperor.	26 June	Crusaders make camp on the Asiatic shore facing Constantinople.
February	Pope lifts excommunication from Crusader army but not from Venetians.	2 July	Emperor Alexios III offers to provision and finance the crusade if it leaves Byzantine territory; Crusader leaders demand Alexios III abdicate in favour of Prince Alexios Angelos.
April	Martin of Pairis arrives in Acre and finds that many Germans have already arrived; there are probably also many Flemings there.	4 July	Crusader leaders decide to attack Constantinople.
7 April	Crusader army evacuates Zadar, whose fortifications the Venetians largely demolish.	5–6 July	Crusaders disembark at Galata, capture Tower of Galata and open defensive chain across the Golden Horn; Venetian fleet enters Golden Horn.
20 April	Crusader fleet sails from Zadar for Corfu; Boniface of Montferrat and Doge Dandalo remain to await Alexios Angelos.	10–16 July	Crusaders besiege Constantinople, focusing on the north-western corner of the city.
25 April	Alexios Angelos arrives at Zadar, then sails for Corfu with Boniface and Dandolo.	17 July	Crusaders assault Blachernae Palace area; Venetians capture a long stretch of the fortifications facing the Golden Horn and start a major fire in the

northern part of the city, but abandon captured walls in order to assist other Crusaders threatened by a feigned attack by Emperor Alexios III.

Night of 17–18 July
People of Constantinople enraged by fire and apparent defeat of Emperor Alexios III, who therefore flees the city.

18 July
Byzantine nobles reinstate Emperor Isaac II, but Crusader leaders insist that Alexios Angelos be made co-emperor.

1 August
Alexios Angelos is crowned as Emperor Alexios IV.

Early August
Alexios VI and a force of Crusaders campaign in Thrace, regaining some territory but failing to capture Alexios III.

18 August
Rioting in Constantinople around this date, Greeks kill some Latin residents of the city.

19 August
Armed Latins (probably refugees from the city) burn a mosque on the southern shore of the Golden Horn and cause a huge urban fire that burns until 21 August.

Summer (April–November)
Muslim ships attack Christian vessels off Cyprus without authorization from the Ayyubid Sultan al-'Adil; ships from Acre retaliate by capturing six Muslim ships off Acre; King Aimery of the (nominal) Crusader Kingdom of Jerusalem declares the truce void and raids Muslim territory in northern Palestine (after 10 September); al-'Adil responds by taking his army to the outskirts of Acre, but does not launch an assault and retires shortly afterwards; plague breaks out in Acre and half the newly arrived Crusader knights die.

Before September
A group of Crusaders, attempting to march from Tripoli to Antioch through Muslim territory near Latakia, are ambushed and many are captured.

August–November
The people of Constantinople begin turning against Alexios IV.

October
Truce agreed around this date between Hospitallers and Muslim ruler of Hims, probably for ten months.

1 December
Conflict erupts between Crusaders and Byzantines.

1204

25 January
Co-Emperor Isaac II dies around this date; rioting in Constantinople; people depose Alexios IV, who turns to Crusaders for support but is imprisoned by the imperial chamberlain, Alexios Doukas, who declares himself Emperor.

5 February
Alexios Doukas crowned as Alexios V.

7 February
Alexios V attempts to negotiate the Crusaders' withdrawal from Byzantine territory, but they refuse to abandon their treaty with Alexios IV.

8 February
Alexios V has Alexios IV strangled; Crusaders decide on full-scale war against Alexios V.

Later in February
Alexios V plans major ambush of Crusader foragers under Henry of Flanders but is defeated.

Spring
Prolonged siege of Ankara by Saljuq ruler Rukn al-Din as part of Saljuq civil war prevents Saljuqs from intervening in confrontation between Fourth Crusade and Byzantine Empire.

March
Crusader and Venetian leaders agree a new treaty, which will divide the Byzantine Empire following their victory.

9 April
Crusader and Venetian forces assault the western half of the Golden Horn fortifications but are repulsed.

12 April	Crusaders launch another assault and gain a foothold within Constantinople.	**24 August**	On expiration of the truce between Hospitallers and the Muslim ruler of Hims, the Hospitallers and Crusaders launch a major raid, which defeats the ruler of Hims and reaches the outskirts of Hama.
Night of 12–13 April	Emperor Alexios V flees from Constantinople.		
13 April	Crusaders and Venetians seize Constantinople and indulge in three days of pillage and massacre.	**September**	Truce between Sultan al-'Adil, the nominal Crusader Kingdom of Jerusalem and the Crusaders; al-'Adil cedes Nazareth, Jaffa, Ramla, Lydda and an area inland from Sidon to the Crusader Kingdom.
May	Sultan al-'Adil is weakened by continuing confrontation with Zangid ruler of Mosul.		
16 May	Baldwin of Flanders is crowned as the first Latin Emperor of Constantinople.		
29 May	A naval attack from Acre against Egypt reaches Fuwa on Rashid branch of the river Nile.		

OPPOSING COMMANDERS

CRUSADER COMMANDERS

Boniface of Montferrat, a younger son of the crusading Marquis William V of Montferrat in north-western Italy, was born early in the 1150s. He was still a teenager when his elder brother Conrad went to Constantinople and, with a hurriedly assembled force of western soldiers, defeated a revolt against Emperor Isaac Angelos. In 1191 Conrad became Marquis of Montferrat; this was the same year that a bitter conflict erupted between the ruling house of Montferrat and the independent neighbouring city of Asti. It would last for 15 years and had more than local significance because Montferrat was widely seen as representing the ideal of feudal aristocratic government while the communal government in Asti was typical of many Lombard towns and cities. Montferrat was also Ghibelline, meaning that it supported the German Holy Roman emperors in their seemingly endless squabbles with the popes and their Guelph supporters.

Raimbaut de Vacqueyras in a late 13th-century French manuscript of famous troubadour songs. Being the only troubadour to achieve knighthood, Raimbaut is shown as a mounted warrior with a lance and shield. (Bibliothèque Nationale, Ms. Fr. 12473, f.60, Paris)

In April 1192 Conrad of Montferrat was assassinated in the Middle East, and Boniface succeeded to the marquisate. Boniface was already a leading supporter of troubadours and the cult of knightly chivalry that they promoted, which encouraged the Provençal troubadour warrior-poet Raimbaut de Vacqueyras to come to Montferrat. Heroic and colourful as Montferrat was, its struggle with Asti ended in failure in 1202. Yet events elsewhere had already thrust Marquis Boniface of Montferrat onto a much broader stage when he was chosen as leader of the Fourth Crusade in summer 1201.

Boniface's decision to accept such a role may have been influenced by his cousin, King Philip of France. At Christmas that year at Hagenau he also met another cousin, Duke Philip of Swabia, King of Germany and claimant to the throne of the Holy Roman Empire. This was when Boniface was introduced to the fugitive Byzantine prince Alexios Angelos. They probably discussed the idea of putting Alexios on the Byzantine throne, and

This manuscript of the epic poem *Eneit* by Heinrich von Veldeke, made in 1215, provides detailed information about German military equipment around the time of the Fourth Crusade. (Staatsbibliothek zu Berlin, Ms. Germ. Fol. 282, f.34, Berlin)

although Boniface of Montferrat was not present at the Crusader siege of Zadar he did support the proposal to divert the crusade to Constantinople. Indeed, as the leading commander of the crusade, the Byzantines expected him to become their new emperor, reportedly hailing him as '*ayos vasileas marchio*' (the Holy Emperor the Marquis). In the event, Baldwin of Flanders was crowned emperor and Boniface had to make do with the crown of Thessaloniki. He had to fight to establish his newly created kingdom, and was ambushed and killed by a Bulgarian force in the foothills of the Rhodope Mountains on 4 September 1207, the faithful troubadour knight Raimbaut de Vacqueyras apparently dying in the same battle.

Count Baldwin IX of Flanders and VI of Hainault was born at Valenciennes in northern France in 1172, the son of Count Baldwin V of Hainault and Countess Margaret of Flanders. He grew up in tumultuous times, becoming count of a wealthy but recently reduced province in 1194. The following year he succeeded his father as Count of Hainault, thus combining the counties under a single ruler. Count Baldwin 'the younger', as he was sometimes known, worked hard to regain various lost provinces in Flanders, and in January 1200 he got King Philip Augustus of France to return most of the very valuable fief of Artois. Only a few weeks after this diplomatic triumph, Count Baldwin took the cross and agreed to take part in Pope Innocent III's new crusade.

In April 1202 Baldwin set out at the head of what was then the biggest contingent of the Fourth Crusade. He also agreed with Boniface of Montferrat and Doge Enrico Dandolo of Venice in their support for the Byzantine prince Alexios Angelos. During the crusade, Count Baldwin of Flanders and his followers played a leading role in the fighting, and after Constantinople fell he was selected as the first Latin Emperor of 'Romania', probably because he had the votes of the Venetians, and was crowned on 16 May.

Early in 1205 the largely Greek-speaking Orthodox population of Thrace rose in revolt against Baldwin's oppressive behaviour and called upon the Bulgarian ruler to help them. The result was a bloody battle outside Adrianople on 14 April 1205, in which Emperor Baldwin was captured. It is now accepted that he died in prison, in unknown circumstances, probably in the Bulgarian capital of Tarnovo, though the Latin Crusaders in Constantinople learned of this only in July 1206. On the other hand rumours later emerged claiming that Baldwin had escaped, and there were even attempts to rescue him.

Doge Enrico Dandolo was born in Venice between 1107 and 1110. As a young man he took part in important embassies to the Byzantine Empire and according to legend – almost certainly untrue – he was blinded by an unnamed Byzantine ruler. The Russian *Novgorod Chronicle* maintained that he had been blinded by 'the Greeks with glass', and that 'his eyes were as though unharmed, but he saw nothing'. In reality his apparent hostility to Byzantium was political and economic.

Elected as doge around April 1192, Enrico Dandolo ruled until his death around 29 May 1205. He was soon involved in prolonged negotiations with Emperor Alexios III, and although his shrewd foresight meant that the Venetians regained many lost trading privileges, the Republic still felt mistreated. This was the situation when, in 1201, Venice agreed to build and man a huge fleet for the forthcoming Fourth Crusade. The doge apparently welcomed the idea of supporting prince Alexios Angelos in order to win the Byzantine throne, perhaps having already discussed the idea earlier. Though old and blind, Doge Enrico Dandolo played a leading and active role in both Crusader assaults on Constantinople in 1203 and 1204. Under a treaty of March 1204 he finally obtained payment of the Venetians' now-huge costs, plus extensive conquered territory. Enrico Dandolo was in Adrianople when Emperor Baldwin was captured by the Bulgarians, and is credited with enabling the remnants of the Crusader army to escape. However, he died very shortly afterwards, probably in Constantinople, and was buried in the huge basilica of the Hagia Sofia.

Lotario de' Conti di Segni, who led the Latin Catholic Church as Pope Innocent III from 1198 until 1216, was born near Anagni around 1160. He came from an aristocratic family and was educated in Paris and Bologna. Having risen within the church hierarchy to become a cardinal deacon in 1190, Lotario de' Conti was elected pope on the death of Celestine III when he was still only 37 years old. Throughout his pontificate he strived to make papal power a political reality rather than merely a legal theory. This would give the papacy the ability as well as the right to impose peace upon temporal rulers, but also give him greater authority to suppress heresy and promote crusades, which he did with enthusiasm.

In the longer term Innocent III's efforts largely failed, but he was undoubtedly very influential, even deposing one of the rival Holy Roman emperors, Otto IV, as well as excommunicating King John of England and other rulers. Nevertheless, Innocent III's policies resulted in widespread civil wars. He was also the leading proponent of the Fourth Crusade and the Albigensian Crusade, both of which probably had a negative impact upon European history.

BYZANTINE COMMANDERS

Emperor Isaac II Angelos ruled the Byzantine Empire from 1187 until 1195, and again more briefly from 1203–04. Born around 1156, he is described as having had a 'bookish' education and even his ascent to the throne was something of a paradox. Having resisted the arrest ordered by Emperor Andronikos I, Isaac Angelos found himself acclaimed as *Basileos* (ruler of the Byzantine Empire) by the people of Constantinople on 12 September 1185. Perhaps because of his own experience of the nobility amongst whom he grew up, Emperor Isaac tended to rely on relatively low-born bureaucrats and foreign soldiers, successfully employing them against aristocratic rebels. While he undoubtedly sold high-ranking positions for money, Isaac also promoted people on merit.

Marriage alliances between Byzantine and other European ruling families had long been common, and Isaac Angelos did the same, taking a daughter of King Béla III of Hungary as his second wife. In his personal life Isaac is said to have preferred an easy life at court but also to be an energetic military campaigner when necessary. He was also accused by the chronicler Nicetas of having a 'mad passion' for building, while similarly being responsible for the demolition of several famous churches and monasteries. Unfortunately, Isaac's policies and the huge problems that the Byzantine Empire faced resulted in very high taxation. This in turn led to resentment, particularly amongst the Vlachs and Bulgarians, who rose in revolt against Byzantine authority. Various other setbacks added to growing discontent, and early in April 1195 Isaac was overthrown and blinded by an aristocratic conspiracy led by his brother, who succeeded him as Emperor Alexios III.

The three other Byzantine rulers at the time of the Fourth Crusade were all named Alexios. The first was Alexios Angelos, who ruled as **Emperor Alexios III** from 1195 to 1203. Born around 1153, he was the elder brother of Emperor Isaac II and spent several years as a prisoner in the County of Tripoli. This was during the reign of the Byzantine Emperor Andronikos I, who was then succeeded by Isaac. Treated well by Emperor Isaac II, Alexios nevertheless conspired against and eventually overthrew his brother. As a ruler, he appears to have been weak-willed, extravagant and lazy, selecting many senior officials on the basis of who could pay most for the position. On the other hand Alexios III had a strong and effective supporter in his wife Euphrosyne and also enjoyed some military success against Balkan rebels, though the credit for this should go to his generals. He also favoured the merchant republics of Pisa and Genoa over their great rival Venice.

After a brief resistance to the Fourth Crusade, Emperor Alexios III fled, after which he wandered around until captured almost by chance by Boniface of Montferrat late in 1204. The ex-emperor was then sent to northern Italy, where he remained until ransomed – or perhaps more accurately purchased –

by Michael I Doukas, the ruler of the Byzantine 'successor state' of Epiros. The unfortunate Alexios III was next sent to Ghiyath al-Din Kaykhusraw I, the Saljuq Sultan of Rum in Anatolia, but when Ghiyath al-Din was defeated by Theodore I Laskaris of Nicaea in 1211 the ex-emperor was again captured. This time he was sent to a monastery, where he died within a year.

The young **Alexios Angelos IV** played a major, if not entirely glorious, role in the Fourth Crusade. Born in 1182 or 1183, the son of Emperor Isaac II Angelos and his first wife, Prince Alexios was apparently left free after the deposition and blinding of his father. Some time during summer or early autumn in 1201 he escaped from Constantinople and made his way to Italy. Failing to gain support there, Alexios Angelos went to Germany, where he was welcomed by his sister Irene, the wife of Philip of Swabia and widow of King Roger III of Sicily. The Byzantine prince was of course at the centre of negotiations about how he might be placed on the imperial throne of Byzantium. During the winter of 1202–03 his envoys and those of Philip of Swabia offered very generous terms to the leaders of the Fourth Crusade, currently camped outside Zadar, if they would support him. Once this had been agreed, Alexios Angelos joined the Crusader army at Corfu in May 1203.

After Alexios III fled and Prince Alexios' blinded and increasingly incapacitated father Isaac II was restored to the Byzantine throne, the Crusaders demanded that Alexios IV become co-emperor. As his father's senility worsened, Alexios IV became the dominant ruler, but it also became clear that he could not repay the Crusaders the amount that had been agreed. The young co-emperor now came under the influence of Byzantine leaders who were deeply hostile to the Crusaders. They included Alexios Doukas, and, as Alexios IV became ever more isolated, it was Alexios Doukas who persuaded him to flee. When the Emperor failed to leave Constantinople, Alexios Doukas first imprisoned him and then had him strangled on or around 8 February 1204.

Alexios V Doukas is often portrayed as a ruthless and bloodthirsty opportunist. In reality he attempted to save the Byzantine Empire, but, because he failed, Alexios Doukas became a villain in the eyes of many. Nicknamed 'Mourtzouphlos', meaning 'bushy or overhanging eyebrows' (this could also be translated as 'melancholy', 'sullen' or 'frowning'), he was a member of the aristocratic Doukas family, though his precise lineage is unknown. Some allege that he had been behind an attempted usurpation by John Comnenos, a member of another prominent aristocratic family, back in 1200. Perhaps that was why Alexios Doukas was in prison when the Fourth Crusade appeared off Constantinople. He was apparently still there when Alexios IV became co-emperor, but was released and made *protovestiarios*, a title that originally indicated the senior official in charge of the imperial wardrobe. Alexios Doukas commanded most of the fighting against the Crusaders outside Constantinople, making him popular in important quarters and facilitating his overthrow of Alexios IV and his coronation as Emperor Alexios V. In particular he won the support of the elite, and by now largely Anglo-Saxon English, Varangian Guard.

During his brief reign Alexios V strengthened the fortifications of the Byzantine capital. Nevertheless, Constantinople eventually fell to Crusader assault and on 12 April 1204 Emperor Alexios V fled to Thrace. There he was captured by the Crusaders, who tried him for treason against Alexios IV and executed him by throwing him from the Column of Theodosios.

OPPOSING FORCES

CRUSADER FORCES

The degree of antipathy between Byzantines and Crusaders during the Fourth Crusade may have been exaggerated. Nevertheless, the Byzantine elite still regarded the Latins or 'Franks' as barbarians having strength, cunning and courage, but lacking the culture that was the mark of a true man. This traditional view was of course out of date by the early 13th century, at least in the more advanced parts of Western Europe where the ideal 'fighting knight' was expected to be literate and cultured.

Although the educated elite of France probably felt no cultural inferiority to the Byzantine Greeks, they were aware that their own sophistication was recent. As the poet Chrétien de Troyes wrote in the later 12th century: 'Our books have told us that Greece was first renowned for chivalry and learning. Then chivalry came to Rome, and all learning, which has now arrived in France.' Similar views were expressed in Germany and Italy.

Religion was, of course, central to both identity and morale in medieval armies. Nor was the idea of Church-sanctioned violence against fellow Christians new. It had been seen in the 'Peace of God' movement, during the struggle between popes and Holy Roman emperors and also against the

Normans in southern Italy. Where armies fighting on behalf of the papacy were concerned, such violence even included the indulgences and remission of sins that were more normally associated with warfare against 'infidel' Muslims and pagans. Even stranger to modern ears was the idea of warriors going off to war in order to avenge 'wrongs done to God', which was prevalent around the time of the Fourth Crusade. For example, the epic *Chanson d'Antioche* has Jesus on the Cross saying to the 'good' robber on his right:

> Friend… the people are not yet born
> Who will come to avenge me with sharp lances,
> And will come to kill the faithless pagans
> Who have always refused my commandments.

In contrast, the knight Robert de Clari's account of the capture of Constantinople reflects the desire, widespread across Europe, for common cause between eastern and western Christianity, which he believed had been undermined by Byzantine treachery.

TOP LEFT
Illustrated in Flanders a few years after the Fourth Crusade, this simple manuscript shows a knight wearing a flat-topped great helm and a horse in full mail barding. (*First Book of Maccabees, Bible de Leau*, Bibliothèque du Grand Séminaire, Ms. 1B3, Liège)

TOP RIGHT
Fully armoured knights in a late 12th-century central-Italian wall painting showing the martyrdom of Thomas Becket. (Church of Sts Giovanni e Paolo, Spoleto)

LEFT
A centaur with a sword, buckler, and pointed helmet on a late 12th-century carving in Studenica Monastery in Serbia. (Author's photograph)

The swords and shields used by humans and mythical creatures on an early 13th-century carved panel in the Cathedral of Freiburg-im-Breisgau reflect south-German infantry equipment at the time of the Fourth Crusade. (Author's photograph)

This said, it is important to recognize that the *chansons de geste* so beloved by the knightly elites included a great deal of parody, social satire and humour. The butt of jokes and targets of social criticism included the pretensions of the knightly class itself, and there is compelling evidence that much of the French-speaking aristocracy did not take the chivalric ideals too seriously, nor their supposed belief in the power of religious relics. The enthusiasm of previously keen Crusaders could also be dampened by the prospect of a sea voyage, though this would not have applied in places like Venice. Such fears were expressed in *Del gran golfe de mar*, a poem by Gauclem Faidit written after his return from the Fourth Crusade, thanking God for saving him from the 'great gulf of the sea' and describing his relief at getting home: 'Nor does a ship shake me about, nor am I frightened by warships.'

While the social status of knights and other ranks may have been changing, laws restricting the use of weapons by lower social classes had also begun to appear. Meanwhile, merchants often seemed to be a class apart, not only armed but being competent in the use of weapons, and it was only during the 13th century that peaceful and portly merchants became commonplace. A short-lived trend in the opposite direction saw monks not only going on crusade but also occasionally taking an active part. This really began when Pope Innocent III announced that anyone could go on crusade, with corresponding changes in certain monastic vows. Yet it remained a passing phenomenon, with monks returning to their original static role by the early 14th century.

The decades leading up to the Fourth Crusade saw significant changes in weaponry and armour. Most obvious was a widespread adoption of the hand-held crossbow. Although the crossbow's slow rate of fire and the speed of the simple hand-held bow (wrongly called a longbow) have both been exaggerated, the crossbow remained a hard-hitting but relatively slow weapon, which proved most effective in siege warfare. The bow was considerably cheaper, but was largely limited to hunters and woodsmen who were themselves relatively few in number.

The Byzantines were clearly surprised by the amount of armour worn by the Crusaders, not just the knights (who may actually have been more lightly protected than the heaviest Byzantine cavalry), but other ranks too, including a large proportion of the infantry. Nicetas Choniates was similarly appalled by the sheer size of the enemy force, which included, he later wrote, 'thousands of archers and crossbowmen, and carried more than a thousand armoured horsemen'. The decade or so before the Fourth Crusade had seen the adoption of increased facial protection in many parts of Europe, though most notably in the south. This trend probably reflected an increased threat from crossbows, which may also have accounted for larger shields and more extensive mail hauberks worn over thick padding.

By the time of the Fourth Crusade the counterweight mangonel or trebuchet was in widespread use in most of Europe, as well as the Middle and Near East. Clearly mentioned in northern Italy in 1199, it was almost certainly known a decade or more earlier, especially in the maritime republics, which were in such close commercial contact with the Islamic world. The counterweight trebuchet had also been used in the Byzantine Empire since the mid-12th century and probably much earlier. During the sieges of Constantinople the Byzantine stone-throwing weapons actually proved more effective, but this was probably because they enjoyed a height advantage.

When it came to intelligence gathering, the Fourth Crusade was operating in a region where such skills were very sophisticated. Although medieval Western Europeans are generally thought to have been inferior to both Byzantines and Muslims in espionage and intelligence gathering, this generalization probably did not apply to Italian maritime republics such as Venice.

Until large numbers of Venetians suddenly took the cross in 1203, the majority of participants in the Fourth Crusade were French or Flemish. In both cases religion was still the primary motivation but elements of the new chivalric code of courtly love were also apparent. One of the verses by a troubadour known as Huon the *châtelain* of Arras, is though to be associated with the Fourth Crusade. It is addressed to the lady he leaves behind and

Most of the ships built by the Venetians for the Fourth Crusade were constructed in private boatyards, as boats still are next to the Rio della Sensa. (Author's photograph)

makes the rather delightful point that, although he leaves his heart with her, he believes that her heart will come with him and that it will make him brave.

Inevitably, more is known about the senior noblemen and significant poets who went on the Fourth Crusade, whereas the rank and file are almost entirely unknown. How they were paid or maintained is similarly obscure, though the army was probably structured along much the same lines as most Western European armies of the time. One of the best documented of these was the army of King Philip Augustus of France. Here the *milites* or knights got 7 *sous* per day while *sergents à cheval* received from 3–4 *sous*. During the early 13th century such mounted sergeants were still a separate cavalry force, usually outnumbering the knights four to one. The *balistarii equites*, or mounted crossbowmen, were paid 5 *sous* a day, compared with the 18 *deniers* a day (1½ *sous*) of the infantry crossbowmen. Infantry sergeants armed with other weapons got only 9 *deniers* (¾ *sou*) a day whereas sappers and miners received 15–18 *deniers* a day according to their skills. Specialist military engineers tended to be highly paid.

Another very important military development was the increasing professionalization of armies, especially in France. This resulted in the employment of large numbers of highly skilled but notoriously violent mercenaries, mostly from Navarre, Flanders, Hainault, Brabant and other parts of the Holy Roman Empire. Most crossbowmen, for example, seem to have been professionals at this time. Other infantry weapons required less skill to use and to maintain, but they could be highly effective in the hands of disciplined foot soldiers. One such weapon was the *jusarme* or *guisarme*, a long-bladed axe with a thrusting point, which the *chansons de geste* usually put in the hands of 'brutish' soldiers, urban militias or peasants. Another infantry weapon that might already have been making its appearance was the *faussart*, which was almost like a single-edged sword-blade mounted on a short haft. For reasons that are still unclear, the *chansons de geste* tend to place maces in the hands of loyal but low-status cavalry and infantry.

The military situation in Flanders was slightly different. Here rapid economic development, urbanization, a decline in the early medieval custom of 'private war' and the church's attempts to ban tournaments meant that the Flemish military had less and less reason to use their skills at home. Furthermore, the spread of free status in other classes of society made 'aristocratic freedom' less distinctive. Another problem for Flemish knights might seem odd, given the growing prosperity of Flanders. This was a worsening lack of money amongst supposedly elite families, which found their income from feudal estates diminishing because of the need to constantly divide such estates amongst their heirs. Similarly the fixed revenues from such estates were devalued by inflation, while at the same time knightly or noble families felt obliged to maintain a traditional but extravagant way of life. Perhaps the crusades opened up other opportunities, as did the demand for mercenaries in France, England and Germany.

The situation was similar in neighbouring Brabant, Namur and Liège, which lay within the Holy Roman Empire. The Brabançons were, in fact, amongst the most feared and respected mercenaries of the later 12th century, particularly as infantry in siege warfare. They also seem to have had a distinctive appearance, as the troubadour Raimbaut de Vacqueyras recalled when, during the siege of Constantinople, he fought on foot 'armed like a Brabantin'. Meanwhile, barding (horse armour) appears to have been quite common in Liège and Hainault, as it was amongst Brabançon mercenary cavalry.

The rest of the largely German Holy Roman Empire was militarily similar to those provinces that now form part of Belgium and the Netherlands. It is, for example, clear that personal display and the wearing of bright colours was almost obligatory for the knightly class, as highlighted in the epic poem *Nibelungenlied*, written around 1200, probably in Austria. Although the *miles* (knights) of Germany were slower to achieve an aristocratic status than their neighbours in much of France, the concept of knighthood came to have a more spiritual or religious element than in France or England. This was because of a close association between the knightly class and the church-ruled mini-states within the empire, as well as the German higher aristocracy's clinging to earlier Carolingian concepts of duty to the church.

Apart from that of Venice, the most important Italian contingent to take part in the Fourth Crusade was probably that of the Marquis of Montferrat. However, it represented only one aspect of the remarkably mixed military forces available in Italy at this time. Apart from significant military differences between northern, central and southern Italy, there were major variations between urban and rural, upland and lowland forces. Those of Montferrat were essentially feudal, rural and came from a region of foothills between the plain of Lombardy

LEFT
Zadar was an important Dalmatian port at the start of the 13th century. Although devastated by the Fourth Crusade, its religious buildings were largely spared, including the circular Church of St Donatus, dating from the 9th century. (Author's photograph)

RIGHT
Venice had difficulty asserting its authority around the Istrian Peninsula before the Fourth Crusade. One of those towns that retained its autonomy for another half-century was Porec (Parenzo), whose Basilica dates back to the 6th century. (Author's photograph)

A carved capital showing a huntsman armed with a sword and leading a dog, made around 1185 in Slovakia, which was then part of the huge medieval Kingdom of Hungary. (*in situ* Praemonstratensian Church, Bina, Slovakia. Jursa photo)

and the Ligurian mountains, where enlistment, command structures and motivations appear to have had more in common with feudal southern France than the increasingly important Italian cities.

It is unclear whether Boniface of Montferrat's infantry were as skilled, disciplined and effective as their better-known rivals from the Lombard cities. As elsewhere, crossbowmen and archers were recruited from the lower ranks of society. Even though the bow was still widely used in Italy it was already becoming a rural and uplands weapon, with the crossbow dominating urban infantry forces. In fact the military importance of trained archers, as distinct from crossbowmen, was already recognized in various parts of Piedmont and Savoy, perhaps including Montferrat, while the first record of such 'corps of archers' would be just two years after the crusade, at Aosta in 1206.

The importance of Venetian military and naval contributions to the Fourth Crusade can hardly be overestimated. In general terms, the early 13th-century Venetian 'art of war' seems to have been similar to that of their Genoese rivals, being based upon a combination of land and sea power. Both these maritime republics relied upon a superior skill in the use of what might be called 'wood-and-rope technologies'. Partly as a result, the lower orders of Venetian society had recognized military roles. In fact, a remarkably broad spectrum of Venetian society was involved in the organization, financing and sponsorship of naval expeditions; this was certainly true of the Fourth Crusade.

During the early days of Venetian history, its military systems were essentially the same as those of other Byzantine provinces in Europe, but this changed considerably during the 12th century. The doge's bodyguard, recorded since the 9th century and perhaps much older, was now supported by an increasingly effective and highly motivated urban militia. Some of the very-limited land area within the Venetian Republic seems to have been held in return for military service, but there was apparently no 'knight's tenure' within Venice itself. Similarly, some Venetian monasteries held land partly in return for supplying military personnel for the doge's guard.

Without the Venetian naval contribution the Fourth Crusade could not have conquered Constantinople. Nevertheless, at the start of the 13th century Venetian naval power was not organized in the same way as in later centuries. Oarsmen in the galleys, like the seamen aboard these and other vessels, were free men, not galley slaves. Nor was work on the galley benches considered demeaning, the oarsmen being chosen by lot to defend their city.

Throughout the medieval period, the Venetian shipbuilding industry relied upon forests in the Istrian peninsula. Great logs were then tied together to be floated along the coast to Venice, where most ships were constructed in private yards. These 'private arsenals' were usually near the owner's home and provided employment when winter prevented fishermen from sailing. Meanwhile the state-owned Arsenal of Venice, initially built around 1104, was primarily used for storage rather than for naval construction, though it did manufacture weaponry.

The Venetian commitment to the Fourth Crusade was massive, but it was not just the Venetian government's money that was involved; large numbers of ordinary people, from merchants to craftsmen, committed their labour and resources. It appears that an agreement to build a ship normally began with the formation of a partnership, with each partner having a share in the vessel. Skilled men would then be hired under one or more master craftsmen. In Genoa, such partners were often unable to pay all these costs without borrowing heavily, sometimes agreeing to repay their creditors out of profits from the ship's first voyage. The net result was that a large part of the Venetian population was depending upon the success of the Fourth Crusade.

Zadar, the first victim of the Fourth Crusade, was currently part of the sprawling joint Kingdom of Hungary and Croatia. Like neighbouring Istria and inland Croatia, Dalmatia was already used to contingents of Crusaders passing through, while local knights had also taken part in such campaigns. In fact Pope Innocent III, the instigator of the Fourth Crusade, was meanwhile promoting crusades against heretics in neighbouring Bosnia; this was a process supported by the archbishops and clergy of several Dalmatian towns, including Zadar. Consequently the population of Zadar tried to protect themselves from the Fourth Crusade by displaying crosses outside their walls.

In strictly military terms, Dalmatia was a mixture of coastal towns organized along lines similar to Italian cities, and a rural hinterland dominated by Byzantine, Slav and Hungarian traditions. Even in Hungary itself, however, Central and Western European military influence was becoming dominant, nine of the 26 aristocratic clans of Hungary being of non-Magyar (non-Hungarian) origin during the reign of King Andrew II (1204–35). In contrast, the Croatian feudal nobility remained notoriously turbulent, often pursuing its own policies with or without Hungarian governmental approval.

BYZANTINE FORCES

The Byzantine Empire is considered to have been a weak military state at the time of the Fourth Crusade, yet this should not be exaggerated. Following catastrophic defeat by the Saljuq Turks at the battle of Manzikert in 1071, it witnessed a remarkable military revival under the Comnenid Emperors (1081–1185). Nevertheless this period also saw an almost equally disastrous Byzantine defeat at the battle of Myriokephalon in 1176, again at the hands of the Saljuqs. Militarily this period remains something of a mystery, some historians regarding the Comnenid revival as superficial while others maintain that the Byzantine Empire became a powerful force and remained so until Emperor Manuel's death in 1180. Thereafter all agree that there was a steep decline.

Organizationally, the Comnenid system was more flexible, less bureaucratic and less centralized than its predecessors. Nevertheless, being something of a 'household government', mirroring aspects of 12th-century Western European government, it also suffered significant weakness in administration, finances and loyalty. Furthermore, by the late 12th century the Byzantine Empire was seriously short of manpower; not just military but also agricultural and economic. Decentralization of authority meant that the emperor was in competition with various regional power centres for military muscle, while a largely unexplained lack of suitably skilled soldiers meant

This 11th-century wall painting in the St Sophia Cathedral in Kiev shows the Byzantine Emperor in the *kathisma* ('Imperial box') of the Hippodrome. (Soviet Academy of Sciences)

that foreigners, either mercenaries or allies, boosted the ranks. Many of these were Westerners, adherents of the Latin Catholic rather than of the Orthodox Church, which was not only the 'state religion' of Byzantium but also provided the empire with its reason to exist.

In more immediate terms, the failure to regain those Anatolian provinces that had once provided the Byzantine army with many of its best troops caused further problems. Isaac II Angelos, whose first reign lasted from 1185 to 1195, was an occasionally energetic military leader but he lost the best parts of his army during unsuccessful campaigns in Bulgaria. His brother, Emperor Alexios III Angelos (1195–1203), apparently made little attempt to rebuild the Byzantine army. Furthermore he allowed the navy, which had been partially revived during the 12th century, to decline disastrously. Even so, the Byzantine army – if not the navy – still existed in 1203, and had fought Saljuq Turks, Vlachs, Bulgars and Kipchaq Turks, albeit with mixed fortunes. Having recently crushed a significant invasion by the Norman Kingdom of Sicily and southern Italy it should theoretically have been able to drive off the smaller Fourth Crusade.

Poor morale was seemingly the Byzantine Empire's greatest problem, and there was already a widespread view in Europe and beyond that the Byzantine Greeks lacked military stamina. The famous Spanish Jewish traveller, Benjamin of Tudela, visited Constantinople only a few years before the Fourth Crusade, subsequently writing: 'They hire from amongst all nations warriors called Loazim [Barbarians] to fight with the Sultan Mas'ud, King of the Tagarmim [Saljuqs], who are called Turks; for the natives are not warlike, but are as women who have no strength to fight.'[3] The dangers inherent in such a situation were recognized in a Byzantine book of advice written a little over a century earlier: 'Do not raise foreigners to high offices nor entrust great

3 Adler, M. N. (tr.), *The Itinerary of Benjamin of Tudela* (Malibu, 1987) p. 71.

responsibilities to them, unless they belong to the royal line of their lands, because by doing so you shall surely render yourself and your Roman officials ineffectual. For whenever you honour a foreigner coming from the herd [a derogatory term for low-class foreigners] as *primicerius* or general, what can you give to a Roman as a worthy position of command?... If you do honour some foreigner beyond [the rank of] spatharocandidatos, from that moment on he becomes a man who will despise you and not serve you properly.'[4]

The concept of 'holy war' was essentially foreign to Byzantine, Orthodox Christian values, though wars could be justified on religious grounds because the emperor and the empire itself were 'holy' defenders of Christianity. Furthermore, the killing of religious rivals was not an intrinsically good action, as it still was to the Crusaders, but was seen as a necessary evil. On the other hand there is strong evidence that, in contrast to this 'official Orthodox Christian ideology', there still existed survivals of 'heroic paganism' within the Byzantine military elites, much of it rooted in pre-Christian, Graeco-Latin warrior mythology. Hence the Scandinavian and Anglo-Saxon warrior attitudes brought to the Byzantine army by the Varangian Guard were not entirely alien.

Another point of contention amongst historians is the importance or otherwise of the *pronoia* (fief) system around this period. This method of donating land as a means of rewarding and maintaining military personal was unlike Western European feudalism because the fiefs in question were not normally passed from father to son. Its significance was also limited because the amount of land the Byzantine emperor had available for donation as *pronoiai* was decreasing; this was because the empire was generally shrinking and because so much land had been donated to the Church. Declining numbers of *paroikoi* 'peasants' to work the land also reduced its value as a means of raising revenue for the state or for *pronoia* holders.

On a more positive note, the Byzantine army was still renowned for strict discipline amongst officers and men, regular and relatively generous pay and

LEFT
The citadel of Trikala in Thessaly is an example of the simple Byzantine fortifications that dotted medieval Greece at the time of the Fourth Crusade. (Author's photograph)

RIGHT
Fragments of 12th- and early 13th-century Byzantine sgraffito-ware ceramics, including serious (G) and satirical (D) subjects: A and B are from Corinth (Archaeological Museum, Corinth); C is from Iznik (Archaeological Museum, Iznik); D is from Verroia (National Archaeological Museum, Athens); E is from the Agora, Athens (Agora Museum, Athens); F is from an unknown location (Louvre Museum, Paris); G is from the Cherson region of Crimea (Hermitage Museum, St Petersburg); H is from Corinth (Archaeological Museum, Corinth).

---

4 Kekaumenos (tr. W. North), 'Logos Nouthetikos, or Oration of Admonition to an Emperor' (De Re Militari website) p. 4.

A mid-13th-century carving around the western door of the Cathedral of St Lawrence in Trogir shows soldiers in Byzantine- or Balkan-style armour. (Author's photograph)

an efficient system of distributing arms, armour and horses at the start of a campaign. The command structure remained theoretically traditional, though recent emperors had been warrior leaders rather than the traditional 'philanthropic bringers of peace'. Unfortunately this also meant that the quality of leadership and command was increasingly dependent upon the personality of the Emperor. Another weakness lay in the fact that 12th- and very early 13th-century emperors were heads of aristocratic clans in which family ties were paramount, and which were often at loggerheads with other clans or families that might have a valid claim to the imperial throne. Worse still, Emperor Isaac II Angelos seems to have given positions of senior military command for political reasons rather than based on the competence of the candidate.

Structurally, the Byzantine army still consisted of indigenous units recruited on regional and often linguistic grounds, plus similarly 'ethnic' units of foreign mercenaries and elite palace or guard regiments. The cavalry were divided into heavily armoured close-combat troopers in a traditional Middle Eastern rather than Western European style, and lightly equipped horse archers, the majority of whom now seem to have been pagan Turks from the steppes or Muslim Turks from Anatolia.

The most famous elite palace regiment was, of course, the Varangian Guard. Originally recruited from Scandinavians and Rus of largely Scandinavian origin, the Varangian Guard now largely consisted of Englishmen of Anglo-Saxon rather than Anglo-Norman origin, plus Frisians, Germans and others. Their duties were remarkably similar to those of the Kievan Russian Druzhina, the Scandinavian *vikinge-lag* and the pre-1066 Anglo-Saxon *huscarls*. Each of these was a mercenary company that served as a ruler's personal bodyguard and the core of a larger army.

In other respects Byzantine military recruitment remained traditional. Emperor Manuel had, for example, settled large numbers of prisoners of war as *paroikoi* peasants with military obligations. Emperor Isaac II then continued his Comnenid predecessors' policy of trying to rebuild a 'national' but not necessarily aristocratic army. Then there were the Armenians. Mistrust between Greeks and Armenians within the Byzantine Empire had been a source of weakness for centuries, but although the Armenians were often politically unreliable, they were regarded as good soldiers. Despite their importance declining during the 12th century, significant numbers of militarily active Armenians were still present in the early 13th century, in both Anatolia and Thrace. Presumably this reflected a traditional Byzantine habit of settling Armenian military colonies close to vulnerable frontiers; those based in the Troad (Troy) region of north-western Anatolia were well-placed to face a continuing Saljuq threat.

Given the parlous state of the Byzantine economy at the start of the 13th century, it is hardly surprising that the number of Western European mercenaries had shrunk. There were still some, perhaps including survivors of those 'Franks' who had defended Varna against Bulgar and Vlach rebels in 1193. However, most of those Westerners who would fight alongside Byzantine troops in defence of Constantinople against the Fourth Crusade seem to have been resident merchants and perhaps ships' crews. The most significant group were the Pisans, who felt a vested interest in supporting the current emperor against what probably looked to them like an invasion by their Venetian commercial rivals.

By the time of the Fourth Crusade, Turkish mercenaries were almost certainly more numerous and more important. They included substantial numbers from the semi-nomadic Turkish peoples of the western steppes, most notably Kipchaqs, who came from the same areas as those Kipchaqs who, with the Vlachs, had instigated the anti-Byzantine revolt that resulted in the recreation of a Bulgarian kingdom.

Other Turkish mercenaries came from Anatolia, including the Saljuq Sultanate of Rum, though the numbers of such troops are believed to have declined after the Byzantine disaster at Myriokephalon in 1176. Perhaps the Byzantine army could no longer afford them. A smaller number arrived as aristocratic political refugees, perhaps with their own military followings. The most important Turkish refugee at the time of the Fourth Crusade was Ghiyath al-Din Kaykhusraw I, youngest son of Sultan Kilij Arslan II by a Christian wife. In 1194–05 he had briefly ruled the Saljuq Sultanate and carried out successful raids against Byzantine territory, but he was then overthrown by one of his half-brothers, Rukn al-Din Sulayman. After wandering around the Middle East, Ghiyath al-Din sought refuge in Constantinople. This was granted by Alexios III, although the Emperor refused to help the refugee Saljuq prince regain his throne. Ghiyath al-Din was still living in Constantinople when the Fourth Crusade arrived.

OPPOSING PLANS

CRUSADER PLANS

The Fourth Crusade was a classic case of plans gone awry, with consequences far from those the planners had intended. Nevertheless, the idea that the assaults upon the Byzantine capital were an accident or a great crime is misleading. This outdated view was perhaps most famously expressed by Steven Runciman, when he wrote that, 'There was never a greater crime against humanity than the Fourth Crusade'. Unfortunately, the view that the entire episode was a gigantic Venetian plot remains deeply rooted. In reality the Crusaders had already developed several fronts during the 12th century, and although previous attacks on Byzantium had not been categorized as crusades, the concept of 'crusades against Schismatic Greeks' was an accepted idea after the Fourth Crusade. In opposition to this 'conspiracy theory' is a now widely accepted 'cock-up theory', which interprets the campaign as a series of unforeseen circumstances. Yet even this is simplistic. Nevertheless, the vulnerability of the Byzantine Empire to invasion had long been known,

The story of the patron saint of Venice, St Mark, in the mosaics of the Cathedral of San Marco, includes illustrations of the ships that made the Republic wealthy and powerful. (Author's photograph)

A number of 11th- or 12th-century bronze chapes, probably for dagger sheaths, have been found in southern England. On one side is a mounted warrior with a kite-shaped shield and a massive axe. This is so unlike the normal military images of that time and place that the owner seems to be declaring, 'I am not a Norman knight!' Might they have been for returning English Varangian Guardsmen?
A – Damaged example (Peter Woods private collection);
B - Complete example (inv. 59.94/45, Museum of London, London)

especially to Venetians, and the suggestions put forward by their leaders during the course of the crusade were certainly not based on ignorance.

What then, did Pope Innocent III hope for when he called for a new crusade? He seems to have been the first major crusade propagandist to recognize the value of current information from the Crusader states. Hence Pope Innocent III sent letters to the leading churchmen of the Latin East, seeking updated political and military assessments of the surrounding Muslim states. Unfortunately for the pope, the Patriarch of Jerusalem did not consider a major crusade to be wise in the existing circumstances. Instead his reply expressed the remarkably optimistic belief that the 'Saracens' were prepared to hand over 'Syria' – perhaps meaning the Holy Land of Palestine – if they were assured that their other possessions would not be invaded.

Sadly, Pope Innocent III disagreed, and promptly published an *encyclical* (papal letter) calling for an expedition to liberate Jerusalem, which had been lost to Saladin back in 1187. Innocent III also delegated legates to prepare the ground, with Cardinal Soffredo going to Venice to organize the necessary naval support and Cardinal Peter Capuano attempting to negotiate peace between the quarrelling rulers of France and England, while two other cardinal legates tried to negotiate an end to the long-standing war between Genoa and Pisa. In the event, neither kings nor emperors took part in the Fourth Crusade, but Pope Innocent III's efforts to promote the expedition lower down the social scale were more successful.

From the start it was obvious that the Byzantine Empire would play a major role in Innocent III's thinking, though not as the crusade's primary target. What the pope apparently had in mind were transit rights, and logistical and perhaps financial support. This, and the pope's impatience with Byzantine caution, was expressed in a letter he sent to Alexios III in November 1199: 'If you wish to wait, because the time of the redemption of that same land is unknown to men, and do nothing by yourself, leaving all things to divine disposition, the Holy Sepulchre may be delivered from the hands of the Saracens without the help of your aid. Therefore through negligence your Imperial Magnificence will incur divine wrath.' However, there is no reason to believe that the pope intended this 'divine wrath' to come in the form of a crusade.

BYZANTINE PLANS

The Byzantine leadership had no real plan, since the idea that the Crusaders should attack them came as a surprise. Nevertheless, the Byzantine army had a long tradition of what might, in modern terms, be called contingency strategies. These were based upon the idea that all means should be used to weaken the enemy, to achieve peace, and to obtain information. Battle was a last resort, and there is no reason to suppose that attitudes had changed by the time of the Fourth Crusade.

Since the Byzantines saw their emperor as the supreme overlord of the Christian world and ruler of a Roman Empire that had been blessed by God, his duty was 'to guard and secure by his ability the powers that he already possesses'. Anything was permissible to achieve this end, and consequently Byzantine behaviour often appeared devious and even duplicitous to outsiders. This was made worse by the weakened Empire's need for allies, including, where necessary, Muslim rulers such as Saladin. In fact the Byzantine Empire's greatest strength was now diplomatic rather than military. The Byzantines feared the Holy Roman Empire in particular, and so they cultivated good relations with Pisa, Genoa, the papacy and Venice. Unfortunately, Emperor Alexios III was unsympathetic to Venetian merchant communities within his own territory, and also overrated the power of the pope. When the crisis came, Pisan support was temporary while that of the Genoese was weakened by recent quarrels.

The result was a sort of paralysis, sometimes sticking to traditional diplomacy, sometimes trying to conciliate the western powers, sometimes doing nothing at all. Not that the Byzantine elite were unaware of the danger. The year before the Fourth Crusade set out, Emperor Alexios III reached a peace agreement with the revived Bulgarian state – previously considered rebels – under which the Byzantines retained lowland Thrace, the Rhodope mountains and Macedonia in return for recognizing Bulgarian independence.

Large numbers of Byzantine manuscripts were sent to Russia to be used in Orthodox Christian religious services, including this psalter dating from the 12th century. (State Public Library, Ms. Gr. 105, St Petersburg)

Since the Byzantine navy had decayed to a shadow of its former self, all that remained beyond a failing diplomacy were fortifications and garrisons. Strong modern fortifications had been erected around the Blachernae Palace in Constantinople only a few decades earlier, and here, unlike the more-famous but also more-archaic fortifications elsewhere in the Byzantine capital, the towers contained smaller chambers with small loopholes rather than large embrasures; perhaps this was to accommodate a new weapon, the crossbow. The towers themselves were also bulkier, probably to support new counterweight trebuchets. The Crusaders would also attack the fortifications along the Golden Horn, which, although considerably weaker than those facing the land, were fronted by open water.

Throughout much of Byzantine history the population of the imperial capital disliked having large numbers of troops within their city. As a result Constantinople was normally lightly defended, given its huge size. Furthermore, the cost of maintaining a substantial garrison was high, whereas threats remained rare. What's more, the presence of large numbers of armed men was seen as a potential threat to the Emperor's throne. Consequently, Byzantine rulers tended to prefer small, elite guard regiments such as the Varangians. When danger did arise, it was normal to assemble troops from neighbouring regions. However, the Fourth Crusade clearly caught the defenders of Constantinople on the wrong foot and there is little evidence of additional troops arriving from elsewhere.

The fortifications defending the northern side of Constantinople faced the Golden Horn and so were not as strong as the landward walls facing west, these being in the Ayvansaray area. (Author's photograph)

THE CAMPAIGN

Accounts of the Fourth Crusade usually start with a tournament held outside the northern French village of Ecry-sur-Aisne on 28 November 1199. Here Counts Thibaud III of Champagne and Louis I of Blois took the cross, promising to go on crusade to regain the Holy City of Jerusalem. Large numbers of other knights followed suit in the excitement that followed such a major medieval 'sporting event'. More senior men followed, including Count Baldwin IX of Flanders on 23 February the following year, Hugh of Saint-Pol, Geoffrey III of Perche and Simon IV of Montfort. Baldwin IX soon made clear that his intention was serious by issuing two important charters for his other territory, the County of Hainault, to make government easier while he was away. In fact they provided the first codification of Hainault's existing 'customary laws' and avoided the outbreaks of private war that had blighted the county in the past.

For all aspiring Crusaders the immediate concerns were money, supplies and transport. Venice seemed to hold the answer, and so six senior men went to negotiate with the Republic's government. All went well, and in April 1201 a treaty was agreed under which the Venetians would transport and provide provisions for 33,500 men and 4,500 horses. In return the leaders of the forthcoming crusade would pay 85,000 silver marks 'on the standard of Cologne' while Venice would also take half of whatever the expedition won. As part of this deal the Venetians would provide – at their own expense – sufficient ships to carry this army, plus 50 galleys to defend it. All would be ready to sail on 29 June 1202, by which time nine months' provisions would also be available.

LEFT
Even before the Fourth Crusade, Venice's Grand Canal was lined with impressive commercial buildings. One of the finest was the Fondaco dei Turchi. (Author's photograph)

RIGHT
The 'Story of Troy', illustrated in Acre in the late 13th century and showing shipbuilders at work. (*Histoire Universelle William of Tyre*, British Library, Ms. Add. 15268, f.105v, London)

The Lido, separating the Venetian Lagoon from the Adriatic Sea, is a popular tourist resort, but at the start of the 13th century it was a sandbar with a few fishermen's huts. (Author's photograph)

It was a massively ambitious undertaking, and for Venice it meant that normal commercial life virtually stopped while all available shipyards were dedicated to preparing the fleet. In fact the Republic did what it had signed up to; it was the Crusaders who proved unable to fulfill their contractual obligations.

Only a month later, the crusade suffered a major blow with the sudden death of its designated leader, Count Thibaud III of Champagne. In his place Marquis Boniface I of Montferrat in Lombardy was chosen as leader and took the cross at a gathering of senior Crusaders at Soissons in August or September 1201. Whether Boniface's troubadour, Raimbaut de Vacqueyras, was present is unknown, but he did celebrate the event in a song, the sixth verse of which proclaimed:

May St Nicholas of Bari guide our fleet,
And let the men of Champagne raise their banner,
And let the Marquis cry 'Montferrat and the lion!'
And the Flemish Count 'Flanders!' as they deal heavy blows;
And let every man strike then with his sword and break his lance,
And we shall easily have routed and slain all the Turks.[5]

Meanwhile the young Byzantine prince Alexios Angelos, son of the deposed, blinded and imprisoned Isaac II Angelos, fled from Constantinople late in September or October 1201, making his way to Sicily and then Rome where he was turned away by Pope Innocent III. Next Prince Alexios went to the court of his brother-in-law, Philip of Swabia, the King of Germany, where, at Christmas 1201, he met the newly elected leader of the forthcoming Crusade, Boniface of Montferrat.

Meanwhile, in the Middle East an internecine war was threatening to tear the Crusader states apart. This 'War of the Antioch Succession' lasted from 1201 until 1216, pitting the Armenian King Leo of Cilicia against Prince Bohemond of Tripoli and Antioch. On the other side of the frontier the

5 'Crusade Song XIX', in J. Linskill, *The Poems of the Troubadour Raimbault de Vaqueiras* (The Hague, 1964) p. 220.

The fortified harbour of Zadar was rebuilt several times, so that little remains of the walls that faced the Fourth Crusade in 1202. (Author's photograph)

Ayyubid realms, which had been torn by dissension following the death of Saladin, were gradually being reunited under the leadership of Sultan al-'Adil of Damascus, who had won control of Egypt in February 1200. Two years later his dominant position was confirmed by winning suzerainty over Aleppo. Then came a massive earthquake, which caused serious damage from Palestine to northern Iraq. Muslim and Crusader fortifications alike suffered, including those of the main Crusader city of Acre.

On the whole the problems in the Middle East might have made the Fourth Crusade's task easier, but it was already facing difficulties even as Crusaders of varying ranks set out in April and May 1202. The agreed assembly point was Venice, and this is where most men headed. However, 29 June 1202, the designated date for setting sail, came and went as contingents large and small straggled into Venice; even Boniface of Montferrat and his followers left home only in early August. Worse still, the numbers reaching Venice were far lower than planned because several contingents decided to make their own way to the Holy Land by different, perhaps cheaper routes. In some cases this was part of the overall plan; the fleet that sailed directly from Flanders under Jean de Nesle, and apparently carrying supplies for the contingents of Counts Baldwin and Henry of Flanders, wintered in Marseilles, having perhaps been slowed by adverse weather. This Flemish fleet then sailed on to the Middle East, along with other contingents from southern France.

Meanwhile the main force encamped on the Lido, the island between the Venetian lagoon and the Adriatic Sea. Its men paid what had been agreed and the great lords dug deep, but the army could offer the Venetians only 51,000 silver marks – nowhere near the agreed sum of 85,000. This meant that Venice faced a financial catastrophe, having dedicated a year's time, effort, materials and lost commerce to the enterprise. As the Crusaders waited on the Lido for men to arrive, they also used up food supplies that Venice had agreed to supply. Autumn and winter passed as all sides faced humiliating failure and financial ruin.

Two lesser-known Venetian sources offer reasonably accurate numbers; Andrea Dandalo maintaining that 4,500 horsemen and 8,000 foot soldiers 'embarked on crusade', whereas the anonymous *Venetiarum Historia* states that Venice transported 5,000 horsemen and 8,000 infantry. Modern statistical methods, based upon the normal ratio of horses to men in a medieval army, and of non-combatants to fighting men, offer significantly larger numbers of mouths to feed; perhaps as many as 1,500 horses, 4,500 knights and squires, plus 10,000–13,750 infantry and servants.

Venice had agreed to provide each person with six *sextaria* (about 3 litres) of flour, grain and vegetables plus half an amphora of wine, as well as three 'Venetian *modia*' (about 25 litres) of feed for each horse. The Venetians could probably support the army for a further three months, but winter would pose really serious problems, the agricultural region between Venice and Cremona probably having been depleted when food was gathered for the Crusaders. Furthermore, summer conditions on the Lido caused disease and desertion.

DIVERSION TO ZADAR

With disaster looming, Doge Enrico Dandolo suggested that Venice would defer the Crusaders' massive debt if the army helped Venice regain the 'rebel' Dalmatian city of Zadar. Payment could then be made once the Crusaders won great victories in the east. Such an idea was fully within accepted medieval concepts of correct feudal behaviour, but the Crusader leadership was also aware that the ordinary Crusaders wanted to fulfil their pilgrimage to the Holy Land – not get caught up in political deals. Once this was agreed, the aged and blind Doge Dandolo took the cross on 8 September 1202 and agreed to lead a Venetian force, which, in an outburst of Crusading enthusiasm, eventually reached around 21,000 men – the largest contingent of the Fourth Crusade.

Zadar was a Latin Catholic city that had pledged its loyalty to King Imre of Hungary, who had himself taken the cross. Hence the Zadar proposal not only caused disquiet in the Crusader ranks but it also upset the Church, and the pope threatened to excommunicate those who attacked Zadar. As if these problems were not enough, around September 1202 Prince Alexios Angelos sent representatives from Verona to the Crusader leadership in Venice, promised to submit the Greek Orthodox Church to papal obedience, provide

At the start of the Fourth Crusade there would have been hundreds of ships in the Lagoon of Venice. (Author's photograph)

the crusade with 200,000 silver marks, provisions for a year, contribute 10,000 mounted soldiers to the expedition and maintain 500 soldiers in the Holy Land. In return he wanted the crusade to overthrow his uncle, the Byzantine Emperor Alexios III.

Such proposals divided the Crusader leadership and were kept secret from the increasingly disgruntled rank and file. However, Boniface of Montferrat, Baldwin of Flanders, Louis of Blois, Hugh of Saint-Pol and Doge Dandolo maintained that the crusade could not afford to turn down such an offer while some senior churchmen also supported them. Boniface and the others therefore signed an agreement with Prince Alexios, in return for which he agreed to join the crusading army at Zadar with his followers before 20 April 1203. News soon reached Alexios III, who sent a letter to the pope, complaining about a feared Crusader assault even before the Fourth Crusade attacked Zadar. Shortly before the Crusader fleet set sail, Boniface of Montferrat headed for Rome to join efforts to smooth relations between the Venetians and Pope Innocent III. Consequently, he was not present when the Crusader leadership decided to support the Venetian assault upon Zadar.

The Fourth Crusade's fleet sailed from Venice in the first week of October 1202, its food supplies almost gone and too late in the year to head for Egypt. At a time when omens were taken very seriously, one of the largest vessels, the *Violet*, carrying Stephen de Perche and his followers, promptly sank, though Stephen survived and later made his own way to the Holy Land. The fleet itself sailed in two divisions, with the main Crusader division going to Pola, where it remained for a few days before heading for Zadar; meanwhile, Doge Dandolo sailed to Piran. The nearby cities of Trieste and Muggia hurriedly sent pledges of loyalty to Venice, after which the doge visited both before heading for Zadar.

The two naval contingents met off Zadar on 10 and 11 November, the armada probably consisting of 50–60 war galleys, 110–150 horse-transporting galleys and an unknown number of other ships, around 50 of which were large *naves* (sailing ships used as transports). An estimated half of the transports and up to two-thirds of the specialist horse-transports had been left in Venice, unwanted and unpaid for.

Major Events of the Fourth Crusade
1. 1202: Crusaders heading for Venice overland are requested not to purchase food at Cremona
2. July–August 1202: Crusader leadership agrees to help Venice recover Zadar
3. Early August 1202: Boniface of Montferrat heads for Venice
4. 8 September 1202: Doge Enrico Dandolo takes the cross
5. September 1202: Alexios agrees to join Crusaders at Zadar before 20 April 1203
6. Early October 1202: Crusader fleet leaves Venice
7. 9 October 1202: Doge Enrico Dandolo's ship arrives at Piran, sails to Trieste then returns via Muggia
8. 10–11 November 1202: Crusader fleets reaches Zadar; Doge Enrico Dandolo rejoins main force at Zadar; November 24: Zadar capitulates
9. November 1202 to April 1203: crusade legates head for Rome; Pope excommunicates the Crusader army
10. November 1202 to April 1203: Crusader army winters at Zadar
11. November 1202 to April 1203: group of Crusaders attempts to travel overland from Zadar in winter
12. November 1202 to April 1203: Simon de Montfort returns to Italy and takes his men to the Holy Land
13. March 1203: Stephen de Perche sails to Acre
14. Spring 1203: Count Renard II of Dampierre sails to Acre
15. Spring 1203: volunteers join Crusader army at Zadar
16. 7 April 1203: Crusader army evacuates Zadar; 20 April: Crusader fleet sails to Corfu
17. 25 April 1203: Alexios Angelos arrives at Zadar then sails to Corfu
18. 24 May 1203: Crusader fleet leaves Corfu
19. May–June 1203: Crusader fleet meets ships returning from Holy Land
20. Early June 1203: Crusader fleet stops at Negroponte (Halkis) where authorities submit to Prince Alexios
21. Early June 1203: Prince Alexios is sent with part of the fleet to Andros
22. Early June 1203: main fleet sails from Negroponte to Abydos, where local authorities surrender
23. Mid-June 1203: expedition under Prince Alexios rejoins main fleet
24. 23 June 1203: Crusader fleet arrives at Agios Stefanos

Other Events
25. 1203: Kipchaqs help Bulgarians expell Hungarians from Brancievo
26. Early June 1203: Emperor Alexios III starts to strengthen the defences of Constantinople
27. 1204: refugees from Zadar regain the city from the Venetians

The Adriatic and Aegean areas, *c*.1202

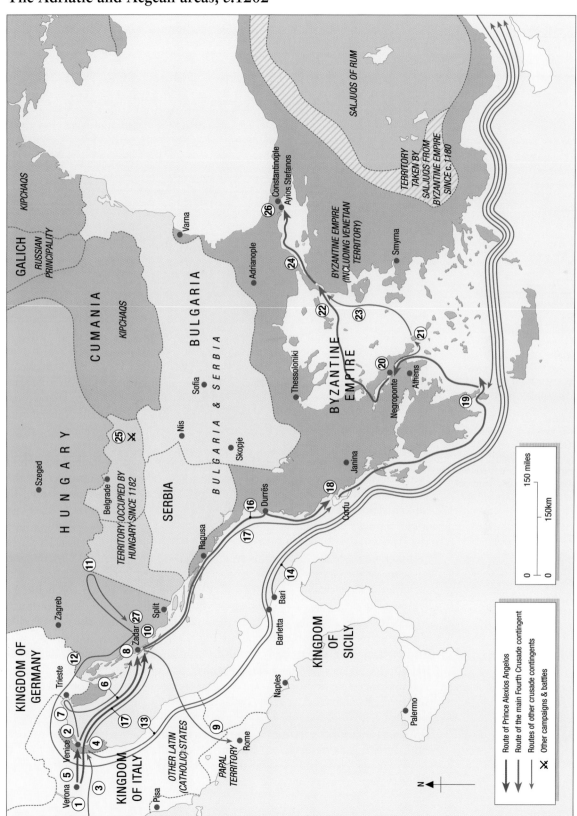

KINGDOM OF GERMANY

GALICH

RUSSIAN PRINCIPALITY

KIPCHAQS

CUMANIA

KIPCHAQS

SALJUQS OF RUM

TERRITORY TAKEN BY BYZANTINE EMPIRE SINCE c. 1180

HUNGARY

Szeged

Zagreb

Trieste

Verona

Venice

Pisa

KINGDOM OF ITALY

OTHER LATIN (CATHOLIC) STATES

Naples

Barletta

Bari

KINGDOM OF SICILY

Palermo

Rome

PAPAL TERRITORY

Split

Zadar

Ragusa

Belgrade

Niš

Skopje

Sofia

SERBIA

BULGARIA & SERBIA

BULGARIA

Varna

Adrianople

Constantinople

Ayios Stefanos

Thessaloniki

Janina

Durrës

Corfu

Negroponte

Athens

Smyrna

BYZANTINE EMPIRE

BYZANTINE EMPIRE (INCLUDING VENETIAN TERRITORY)

TERRITORY OCCUPIED BY HUNGARY SINCE 1182

Route of Prince Alexios Angelos

Route of the main Fourth Crusade contingent

Routes of other crusade contingents

Other campaigns & battles

0 — 150 miles

0 — 150 km

N

47

The leaders of Zadar were reportedly prepared to surrender but others 'within the army' believed that the pope's warning would stop the Crusaders attacking. Indeed the people of Zadar hung crosses outside their walls to show that they were not only Christians but Crusaders. Nevertheless Archbishop Thomas of the rival city of Split, farther down the Dalmatian coast, blamed Zadar for the attack, claiming that many of its leading citizens had protected or helped Bosnian heretics and that they were themselves polluted by heresy. Many in the Crusader host were unhappy about this confrontation and held back, but the majority joined the Venetians' siege, which was brief and brutal.

According to Robert of Clari: 'When the Doge saw that the barons would aid him he caused his engines to be set up to assault the city, until they of the city saw that they could not hold out against them; then they came to terms and surrendered the city to them'.[6] The date was 24 November 1202. How much damage was done at this stage is unclear, but an Italian source called the *Memorie della Dalmazia* stated that: 'After the desolation of Zara [Zadar], many of the inhabitants sought refuge in the interior of Croatia, and on some of the islands'.

For their part the Crusaders and Venetians settled down to spend the winter in the conquered city, which provided plenty of shelter but not much food. At some unspecified date that winter the pope took the remarkably drastic step of excommunicating an entire Crusader army. Given this it is hardly surprisingly that many Crusaders, including some senior men, either abandoned the crusade or made their own way to the Holy Land. However, the majority remained in Zadar, where the army received some welcome reinforcements, including Pierre de Bracheux, a knight who had not travelled with his feudal lord Louis of Blois but who would play a prominent role in the crusade and its aftermath. During that winter, negotiations continued with Prince Alexios Angelos, and in January these culminated in a formal treaty by which the leaders of the Fourth Crusade agreed to help Prince Alexios become ruler of the Byzantine Empire.

6 Clari, Robert de (ed. Edward N. Stone), *Three Old French Chronicles of the Crusades* (Seattle, 1939).

Being excommunicated was an uncomfortable position for medieval people and they were eager to have the pope's ban lifted. In February 1203 he did so, albeit on the understanding that the Crusader leaders made full restitution to the King of Hungary and swore not to attack Christians. This was accepted by all except the Venetians, who refused to admit wrongdoing and therefore remained excommunicated.

The Crusaders remained in Corfu for some time while their leaders argued about whether to go to Constantinople or head for Egypt. (Author's photograph)

Not surprisingly, the Crusader leadership tried to keep the rank and file ignorant of this continued Venetian excommunication. On 7 April 1203 the Crusader army evacuated Zadar and the Venetians razed its fortifications. This done, the Crusader armada set sail on 20 April, 'destitute of goods' according to a contemporary chronicler known as the 'Anonymous of Halberstadt'; in other words they were still seriously short of food. Boniface and Dandolo stayed behind to await Prince Alexios Angelos. After a brief pause at Dürres in Albania, the fleet reached Corfu, news of its approach having reached Emperor Alexios III. According to the chronicler Nicetas: 'He began to repair the rotting and worm-eaten small skiffs, barely twenty in number, and making the rounds of the City's walls, he ordered the dwellings outside pulled down.'[7] The 'twenty small skiffs' were probably the ships that would be tied alongside the boom across the entrance to the Golden Horn.

The stay in Corfu was something of a make-or-break time for the Fourth Crusade, the majority of men strongly opposed to the idea of diverting to Constantinople. After Boniface, the Doge and Prince Alexios rejoined them, the prince's offers of substantial Byzantine assistance seeming to solve the food problem. Furthermore, their leaders promised that the army would stay in Constantinople for only a month before continuing to the Holy Land, unless the men freely consented to an extension. The argument was bitter and prolonged, but in the end a decision was made – the Fourth Crusade would sail to the Byzantine capital and support Prince Alexios Angelos in his claim to the imperial purple.

7 Choniates, Nicetas (tr. H. J. Magoulias), *O City of Byzantium, Annals of Nicetas Choniates* (Detroit, 1984) pp. 296–97.

Operations around Constantinople and Thrace

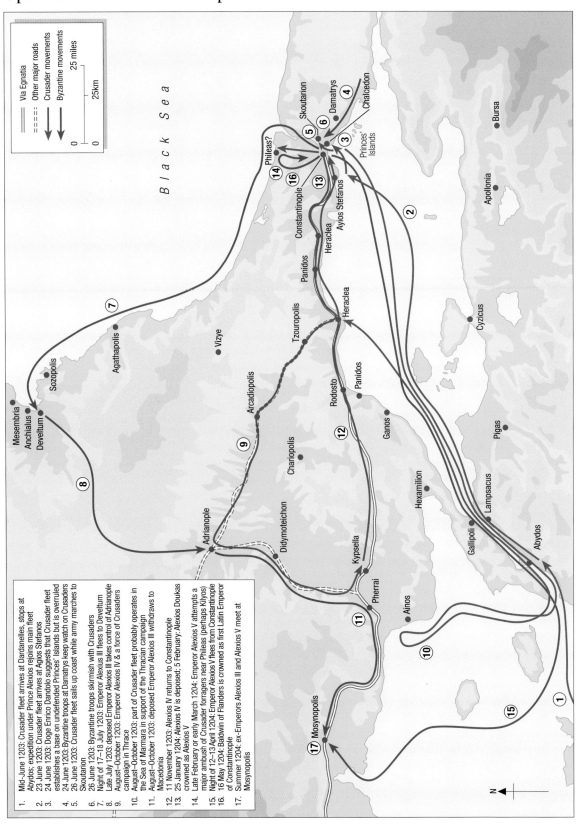

1. Mid-June 1203: Crusader fleet arrives at Dardanelles, stops at Abydos; expedition under Prince Alexios rejoins main fleet
2. 23 June 1203: Crusader fleet arrives at Agios Stefanos
3. 24 June 1203: Doge Enrico Dandolo suggests that Crusader fleet establishes a base on undefended Princes' Islands but is overruled
4. 24 June 1203: Byzantine troops at Damatrys keep watch on Crusaders
5. 26 June 1203: Crusader fleet sails up coast while army marches to Skoutarion
6. 26 June 1203: Byzantine troops skirmish with Crusaders
7. Night of 17–18 July 1203: Emperor Alexius III flees to Develtum
8. Late July 1203: deposed Emperor Alexios III takes control of Adrianople
9. August–October 1203: Emperor Alexios IV & a force of Crusaders campaign in Thrace
10. August–October 1203: part of Crusader fleet probably operates in the Sea of Marmara in support of the Thracian campaign
11. August–October 1203: deposed Emperor Alexios III withdraws to Macedonia
12. 11 November 1203: Alexios IV returns to Constantinople
13. 25 January 1204: Alexios IV is deposed; 5 February: Alexios Doukas crowned as Alexios V
14. Late February or early March 1204: Emperor Alexios V attempts a major ambush of Crusader forragers near Phileas (perhaps Kilyos)
15. Night of 12–13 April 1204: Emperor Alexios V flees from Constantinople
16. 16 May 1204: Baldwin of Flanders is crowned as first Latin Emperor of Constantinople
17. Summer 1204: ex-Emperors Alexios III and Alexios V meet at Mosynopolis

Believing that Prince Alexios would be accepted by the Byzantine populace, the Crusaders sailed along the seaward walls of Constantinople. (Author's photograph)

THE FIRST ASSAULT ON CONSTANTINOPLE

On 24 May 1203 the fleet left Corfu. The Crusader fleet now headed into the Aegean, stopping at Halkis, where the local authorities submitted to Prince Alexios Angelos. This so encouraged the Crusader leadership that they sent Alexios and several ships to extend his authority over the neighbouring island of Andros, where, however, the locals resisted for some time. These ships then headed northwards to rejoin the rest of the fleet at Abydos in the Dardanelles in mid-June. The local authorities surrendered to prevent their town being looted, so the hungry Crusaders were obliged to forage over a wide area. After leaving the Dardanelles, the Crusader fleet arrived off Agios Stefanos (Yesilköy) just west of Constantinople on 23 June. Rather than coming ashore on the European side, it sailed on the following day past the Princes' Islands, which Doge Dandolo had suggested as a suitable base, to Chalcedon (Kadıköy) on the Asiatic side of the southern entrance to the Bosporus. There the army disembarked, probably taking over a day to organize itself and exercise the horses. Nicetas seems to indicate that the galleys promptly made for Skoutarion (Üsküdar) where they could cover the disembarkation, but Crusader sources suggest that they remained closer to the transports.

On 26 June the Crusader army marched up the coast while the fleet sailed alongside. Nicetas describes a half-hearted Byzantine resistance on the Anatolian shore: 'The Romans who appeared on the nearby hills and stood along the shore discharged missiles against the warships, but to no avail… Another contingent kept watch to the north around Damatrys (Samandra)… they made no attempt to attack the enemy forces, and when the latter charged them, they rose up and scattered.'[8] The Fourth Crusade now made camp at Skoutarion, facing Constantinople across the narrow Bosporus.

Aware that the initial reason for the diversion of the Fourth Crusade had been a shortage of food, on 2 July Emperor Alexios III offered to feed and finance the Crusaders if they left Byzantine territory. However, the Crusader leaders maintained their support for Prince Alexios Angelos and demanded that the Emperor abdicate. Apparently believing that the people of Constantinople

8 Ibid., p. 297.

LEFT
The Dardanelles narrow to a channel just 2km wide at Lapseki. (Author's photograph)

RIGHT
Gallipoli was the main naval base defending the Dardanelles, though the few remaining Byzantine warships made no effort to challenge the Fourth Crusade as it sailed past. (Author's photograph)

BOTTOM
After sailing into the Bosporus, the Crusader fleet moored at Chrysopolis (Üskudar), from where they had a clear view of the Byzantine capital. (Author's photograph)

were being kept in the dark about the Prince's presence, they sent young Alexios with ten galleys close to the city's seaward walls, where they called upon the Byzantines to rise up in his favour. After rowing back and forth for a while, receiving insults and missiles, the attempt was abandoned.

Rather than admit that Prince Alexios lacked the support he claimed and accept Emperor Alexios III's offer of aid, the leaders – now apparently supported by most of the army – chose to press Prince Alexios' case militarily. The fact that their forces were in an ideal location to attack Galata and the Golden Horn leaves open the possibility that they considered doing so all along. To appreciate the advantages of the Crusader position, the hydrography of the medieval Bosporus must be understood. In July vast quantities of water from the spring thaw in Russia and Ukraine flowed into the Black Sea, through the Bosporus, the Sea of Marmara and the Dardanelles, into the Aegean and Mediterranean. Though the current was at its strongest, it was weaker close to the coasts, and along the western shore facing Üsküdar there was actually a weak, northwards-flowing counter-current, beyond which was a beach suitable for a naval landing.

The standard *uissiers*, the Mediterranean horse-transports of this period, carried 30 animals, though the majority of warhorses in the Crusader army were transported aboard less-specialized vessels. The horse-transports would have dropped anchor close offshore, been backed up until the stern was grounded, and then made fast with a cable.[9] Each vessel would also have required about 50m of shoreline, in addition to which the Crusaders sent boats carrying crossbowmen to clear defenders from the beach. Normal wind conditions at this time of year were also helpful to the Crusaders, usually blowing moderately from the north or north-east.

The galleys and *uissiers* were boarded early in the morning of 5 July, setting off to the sounds of, 'trumpets of silver and of brass, as many as an hundred pair of them, and tabours and timbrels in great number' according to Robert de Clari. Emperor Alexios III had not been idle, sending a substantial force of cavalry and infantry to defend the area. Nevertheless, Byzantine resistance was completely ineffective, and, according to Hugh of St Pol, 'The Greeks fled before them when they landed and the army came to the Tower of Galata'. Robert de Clari added that the defenders were chased 'as far as a bridge which stood nigh the end of the city, and above this bridge was a gate, through which the Greeks passed inward and fled into Constantinople'. This was probably a floating causeway over the narrow upper part of the Golden Horn close to the Monastery of Sts Kosmas and Damian.

Unfortified Galata apparently fell at once, its inhabitants largely being non-Byzantine merchant communities. Nevertheless, there was a significant fire on 5 July. Down by the Golden Horn stood a substantial fortification called the Galata Tower, not to be confused with the existing Galata Tower, which is higher up the hill. It served as an anchorage point for the northern end of a floating defensive boom. Rather than assault the boom itself, the Crusaders decided to attack this Galata Tower, which stood approximately on the site of today's Yalata Camii Serifi mosque. It had a substantial garrison, including Englishmen, Pisans from the resident merchant community, Geneviani (who were probably Genoese) and Dacians (who may have been Hungarians or Kipchaqs).

Once the Crusader cavalry returned from their pursuit, the army re-formed while some galleys beached close enough for their stone-throwing machines to bombard the tower, which was also assaulted from the land.

LEFT
When the Fourth Crusade reached the Bosporus its fleet made landfall on the eastern shore at Chalcedon (Kadiköy). (Author's photograph)

RIGHT
The suburb of Galata lies on the north side of the entrance to the Golden Horn. From here a floating boom was stretched across the harbour entrance during emergencies. (Author's photograph)

9 Pryor, J. H., 'The Chain of the Golden Horn, 5–7 July 1203' in I. Shagrir (ed.), *In Laudem Hierosolymitani: Studies in Crusades and Medieval Culture in Honour of Benjamin Z. Kedar* (Aldershot, 2007) p. 377.

BREAKING THE GOLDEN HORN CHAIN, 5 OR 6 JULY 1203 (pp. 54–55)

A floating chain or boom closed the entrance to the Golden Horn in an emergency, its northern anchorage point being protected by a strongly garrisoned fortification known as the Tower of Galata. After taking control of the suburb of Galata and setting much of it on fire, the Crusaders and Venetians attacked this tower. The Venetians also ran some of their galleys ashore just east so their light 'siege engines' could force the Byzantine defenders to keep their heads down.

After a bitter struggle the Crusaders captured the Tower of Galata while some of its garrison escaped across an unstable walkway on top of the floating boom. Others sought refuge in old Byzantine ships, which had been moored alongside the boom, but many are said to have drowned in the Golden Horn. Once inside the Tower of Galata the Crusaders either disconnected or broke the northern attachment of the floating boom, which then drifted away on the current. This enabled the Venetian fleet to enter the Golden Horn and capture or destroy the Byzantine ships they found there.

Once the Venetian fleet broke into the Golden Horn it attacked the Byzantine ships taking shelter there, capturing many, while others ran themselves ashore. (Author's photograph)

This struggle proved fierce but one-sided, and on 6 July the Galata Tower was taken by storm. The Byzantine chronicler Nicetas seems to have observed events from Constantinople, writing: 'It was a sight to behold the defenders fleeing after a brief resistance. Some were slain or taken alive, and others slid down the chain as though it were a rope and boarded the Roman triremes, while many others lost their grip and fell headlong into the deep'.

The Crusaders now had command of the northern end of the boom or chain across the Golden Horn. This remarkable device was about 750m long and consisted of a massive iron chain supported by large floating timbers with a flexible walkway on top. A number of Byzantine ships were also moored along its inner side to serve as defensive positions. The Crusaders probably unfastened rather than broke the northern end of the boom after seizing control of the Gatala Tower. A claim that a big ship named the *Aquila* rammed and broke the boom is very unlikely, though Venetian vessels now entered, capturing, burning or driving ashore the Byzantine vessels within the Golden Horn.

Unlike the Ottoman army that conquered Constantinople in 1453, the Fourth Crusade was relatively few in number and its leaders knew that they would have to focus any attacks upon a limited part of the city's defences. They selected the north-western corner, where the Crusaders could assault the landward walls of the Blachernae Palace while the Venetian fleet attacked the western end of the Golden Horn walls. The Crusaders therefore crossed the Horn on 10 or 11 July, presumably via the bridge previously used by retreating Byzantine troops. Here, according to Nicetas, 'they met some slight resistance from the Romans around the bridge located nearby and around the place called Trypetos Lithos [Pierced Stone]'.

The Crusaders then made camp and established a siege position facing the Blachernae Palace. According to Nicetas the camp was 'divided in part into trenches and wooden palisades around a hill… The defenders on the wall could see the raised tents and could almost converse with those within who faced Gyrolimne [a land gate immediately west of the palace].' Meanwhile, the Venetians erected siege engines and scaling ladders aboard some of their ships.

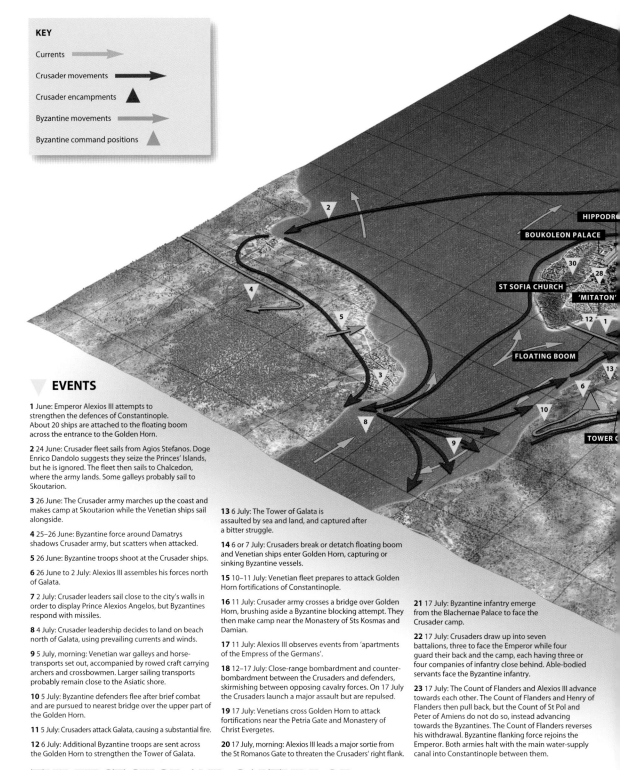

KEY

Currents

Crusader movements

Crusader encampments

Byzantine movements

Byzantine command positions

HIPPODR

BOUKOLEON PALACE

30

28

ST SOFIA CHURCH

'MITATON'

12   1

FLOATING BOOM

13

6

10

TOWER

2

4

5

3

8

9

▽ EVENTS

1 June: Emperor Alexios III attempts to strengthen the defences of Constantinople. About 20 ships are attached to the floating boom across the entrance to the Golden Horn.

2 24 June: Crusader fleet sails from Agios Stefanos. Doge Enrico Dandolo suggests they seize the Princes' Islands, but he is ignored. The fleet then sails to Chalcedon, where the army lands. Some galleys probably sail to Skoutarion.

3 26 June: The Crusader army marches up the coast and makes camp at Skoutarion while the Venetian ships sail alongside.

4 25–26 June: Byzantine force around Damatrys shadows Crusader army, but scatters when attacked.

5 26 June: Byzantine troops shoot at the Crusader ships.

6 26 June to 2 July: Alexios III assembles his forces north of Galata.

7 2 July: Crusader leaders sail close to the city's walls in order to display Prince Alexios Angelos, but Byzantines respond with missiles.

8 4 July: Crusader leadership decides to land on beach north of Galata, using prevailing currents and winds.

9 5 July, morning: Venetian war galleys and horse-transports set out, accompanied by rowed craft carrying archers and crossbowmen. Larger sailing transports probably remain close to the Asiatic shore.

10 5 July: Byzantine defenders flee after brief combat and are pursued to nearest bridge over the upper part of the Golden Horn.

11 5 July: Crusaders attack Galata, causing a substantial fire.

12 6 July: Additional Byzantine troops are sent across the Golden Horn to strengthen the Tower of Galata.

13 6 July: The Tower of Galata is assaulted by sea and land, and captured after a bitter struggle.

14 6 or 7 July: Crusaders break or detatch floating boom and Venetian ships enter Golden Horn, capturing or sinking Byzantine vessels.

15 10–11 July: Venetian fleet prepares to attack Golden Horn fortifications of Constantinople.

16 11 July: Crusader army crosses a bridge over Golden Horn, brushing aside a Byzantine blocking attempt. They then make camp near the Monastery of Sts Kosmas and Damian.

17 11 July: Alexios III observes events from 'apartments of the Empress of the Germans'.

18 12–17 July: Close-range bombardment and counter-bombardment between the Crusaders and defenders, skirmishing between opposing cavalry forces. On 17 July the Crusaders launch a major assault but are repulsed.

19 17 July: Venetians cross Golden Horn to attack fortifications near the Petria Gate and Monastery of Christ Evergetes.

20 17 July, morning: Alexios III leads a major sortie from the St Romanos Gate to threaten the Crusaders' right flank.

21 17 July: Byzantine infantry emerge from the Blachernae Palace to face the Crusader camp.

22 17 July: Crusaders draw up into seven battalions, three to face the Emperor while four guard their back and the camp, each having three or four companies of infantry close behind. Able-bodied servants face the Byzantine infantry.

23 17 July: The Count of Flanders and Alexios III advance towards each other. The Count of Flanders and Henry of Flanders then pull back, but the Count of St Pol and Peter of Amiens do not do so, instead advancing towards the Byzantines. The Count of Flanders reverses his withdrawal. Byzantine flanking force rejoins the Emperor. Both armies halt with the main water-supply canal into Constantinople between them.

THE FIRST SIEGE AND CAPTURE OF CONSTANTINOPLE, 23 JUNE TO 18 JULY 1203

The Crusaders arrived outside the Byzantine capital expecting Prince Alexios Angelos to be welcomed by the people, and when he was not they attacked the city, eventually forcing the Byzantines to accept a new ruler.

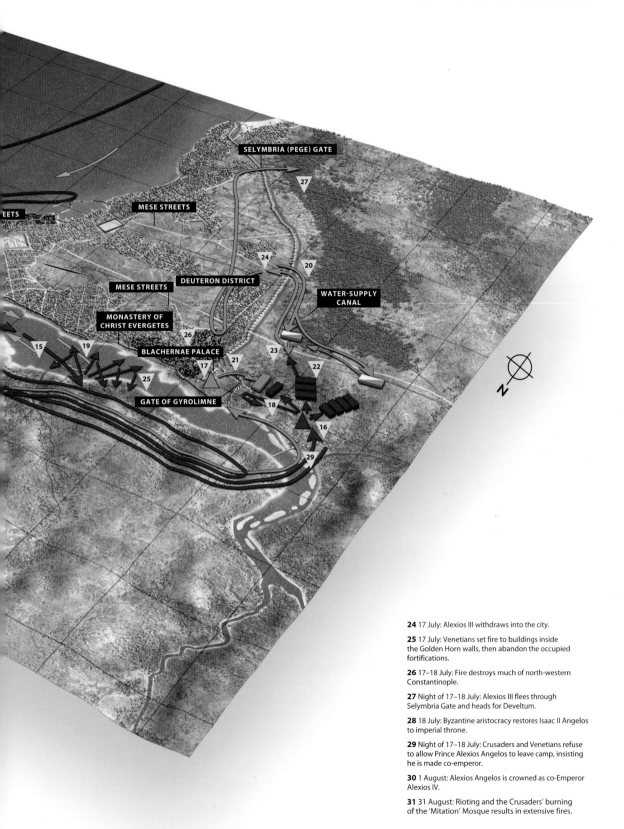

SELYMBRIA (PEGE) GATE

MESE STREETS

EETS

MESE STREETS

DEUTERON DISTRICT

WATER-SUPPLY CANAL

MONASTERY OF CHRIST EVERGETES

BLACHERNAE PALACE

GATE OF GYROLIMNE

24 17 July: Alexios III withdraws into the city.

25 17 July: Venetians set fire to buildings inside the Golden Horn walls, then abandon the occupied fortifications.

26 17–18 July: Fire destroys much of north-western Constantinople.

27 Night of 17–18 July: Alexios III flees through Selymbria Gate and heads for Develtum.

28 18 July: Byzantine aristocracy restores Isaac II Angelos to imperial throne.

29 Night of 17–18 July: Crusaders and Venetians refuse to allow Prince Alexios Angelos to leave camp, insisting he is made co-emperor.

30 1 August: Alexios Angelos is crowned as co-Emperor Alexios IV.

31 31 August: Rioting and the Crusaders' burning of the 'Mitation' Mosque results in extensive fires.

For about a week the two sides bombarded each other with stone-throwing siege machines, those of the Crusaders reaching the palace and those of the defenders reaching the besiegers' tents. Nicetas seems to have been particularly shocked by Emperor Alexios III's lack of action, and the Byzantine defenders do seem to have lacked coordinated leadership rather than courage. In Nicetas' words, 'both sides mounted special cavalry charges many times during the day, and knight competed with horseman in the throwing of the javelin with the excitement and zeal wrought by bravery'.

The first major assault was directed against the Blachernae Palace on 17 July, but the Crusaders were defeated, substantial losses being inflicted by Pisans, Englishmen and Danes in Byzantine service. Raimbaut de Vacqueyras was with Boniface of Montferrat's unit and took part in these early attacks, as recounted in his *Epic Letter*:

> By the Blachernae, beneath your banner,
> I stood armed, like a Brabantine,
> With helm and hauberk and stout gambeson.

Raimbaut would also take part in the siege of 1204 and his letter asks the Marquis for a reward for the injury he suffered in that assault:

> And I fought beneath the tower in the Petrion,
> And there was wounded beneath my armour.[10]

Robert de Clari was particularly impressed by the siege machines that the Venetians brought to bear:

> He [Doge Dandolo] had them take the spars which support the sails of the ships, which were full thirty fathoms in length, or more, and these he caused to be firmly bound and made fast to the masts with good cords, and good bridges to be laid on these and good guards alongside them, likewise of cords; and the bridge was so wide that three armed knights could pass over it abreast. And the Doge caused the bridge to be so well furnished and covered on the sides with sailcloth and other thick stuff, that those who should go up the bridge to make an assault need have no care for crossbow bolts nor for arrows.

10 Linskill, J., *The Poems of the Troubadour Raimbault de Vaqueiras* (The Hague, 1964) p. 310.

Nicetas was similarly impressed, recording that: 'The ships were covered with ox hides to make them impervious to fire, and the halyards were fashioned into scaling ladders with rungs made of rope and lowered and again raised high by cables bound to the masts... They then engaged the defenders on the towers and easily routed them, since they were fighting from a higher vantage point and discharging their missiles from above.' This was clearly why the Venetian assault was more successful that the Crusaders' attack on the landward walls, winning control of 25–30 towers facing the Golden Horn.

In this crisis Emperor Alexios III took drastic action and led a large sortie against the Crusader flank. It proved a tactical success but had an unfortunate impact upon the Byzantines' already fragile morale. Early on 17 July Emperor Alexios III emerged at the head of a substantial force through the Gate of St Romanos, south of the river Lycus. Nicetas remained unsympathetic: 'When the opponent's land forces suddenly beheld this huge array, they shuddered. Indeed, a work of deliverance would have been wrought had the emperor's troops moved in one body against the enemy, but now the nagging idea of flight and the faintheartedness of those about him thwarted Alexios from what needed to be done.'

Robert de Clari provides a detailed review of the Byzantine force, which consisted of 17 battalions, but exaggerates their numbers. The larger part went to threaten the Crusader encampment and the flank of the Crusader cavalry, who drew up to face the Emperor. A substantial infantry force similarly emerged, to draw up between the fortifications and the Crusader camp. Anticipating a full-scale battle, the Count of Flanders placed his battalion in the vanguard, the second being the men of the Count of Saint-Pol and Lord Peter of Amiens and the third that of Henry of Hainault and the Germans. Each cavalry unit was closely followed by three or four units of 'infantry sergeants' from the same country as the horsemen. Meanwhile four other battalions formed a reserve to protect the encampment. Boniface of Montferrat had overall command, and of the first battalion in this rearguard.

The northern end of the ancient landward walls of Constantinople were extended in the 12th century to enclose the Blachernae Palace, and incorporated several more modern ideas. (Author's photograph)

Next came Count Louis of Blois, the knights of Champagne and the knights of Burgundy. These rearguard battalions had strict orders to stay in place unless the advancing battalions were clearly defeated. Meanwhile every other man, including 'grooms and kitchen-knaves', took whatever arms and armour they could find and were arrayed facing the Byzantine infantry.

The confrontation between the Crusader and Byzantine cavalry is described in great detail by Robert de Clari, though his interpretation of the result might be misleading. Apparently the Count of Flanders and Emperor Alexios III advanced towards each other, starting about 'a quarter of a league' (about 1km) apart. The battalions of the Count of St Pol and of Henry of Hainault followed with their respective infantry 'at the tails of the horses'. When the Count of Flanders had advanced 'full two crossbow shots' his counsellors warned that he was in danger of being cut off by the other enemy cavalry on his right flank, so he turned back, as did his brother Henry. However, the troops of the Count of St Pol and Lord Peter of Amiens shouted, 'Lord! Lord! The Count of Flanders turneth back! And since he turned back, he left to you the vanguard. Now let us take it, in God's name!' Refusing Baldwin of Flanders' urgent requests for them to pull back, they continued to

advance. This virtually forced Baldwin to do the same, and resulted in a slow and somewhat disorganized Crusader charge by both cavalry and accompanying infantry.

Soon the two armies were close enough for archers and crossbowmen to exchange shots. Yet there was still a small hillock between them, which the Crusaders reached first. At this point Emperor Alexios III halted his army and was rejoined by the Byzantine battalions, which had been threatening the Crusader camp. In reality it is more likely that the Crusaders rather than the Byzantines were now 'dismayed', being far from their rearguard and palisaded encampment. There was still a 'great canal' lying between the armies, this being the conduit that carried drinking water into Constantinople. It was thought dangerous to cross, so the Crusader leaders took council.

In the event, Alexios III decided the outcome by withdrawing into the city's fortifications. Tactically his sortie had worked. The Venetians had abandoned their gains in order to support the Crusaders but had set fire to buildings next to the Golden Horn walls. This soon got out of control, spreading deep into the built-up area and probably contributing to Alexios III's decision to pull back. This first fire within Constantinople burned until 18 July and destroyed an estimated 1,250,000m².

By the end of 17 July the besiegers had suffered heavy casualties with nothing to show for it. However, unknown to them, the disastrous fire and the Emperor's retreat so enraged Constantinople's population that Alexios III lost support within the Byzantine aristocracy and army. Taking 'one thousand pounds of gold and other imperial ornaments made of precious gems and translucent pearls', Emperor Alexios III fled during the night and headed for Develtum, a fortified town on the Gulf of Burgas. The Byzantine court now reinstated Isaac II, but the Crusaders, surprised by this turn of events, insisted that Isaac II's son, Prince Alexios, be made co-emperor, and that both rulers did what Alexios had promised months before. Eventually the Byzantines agreed, and on 1 August 1203 he was crowned as Alexios IV. The Fourth Crusade's diversion looked like a success.

TOTTERING TOWARDS CONFRONTATION

In fact the Byzantine government was in no position to supply the funds, food and military support that had been promised in its name, though an initial payment was enough for the Crusaders to pay their debts to the Venetians. Instead the co-emperors started confiscating church treasures, which made them very unpopular with ordinary people. In contrast, the Greek Orthodox Church leadership apparently making no protest because, in Nicetas' opinion, 'They had been taught to fawn, like Maltese spaniels'.

As weeks passed into months, the leaderships on both sides found themselves in an increasingly difficult position. The Crusader leaders were unable or unwilling to fulfill the promise to their followers that the crusade would press on towards the Holy Land, while the co-emperors Isaac II and Alexios IV were caught between the demands of their people and those of the Crusaders. Meanwhile there were those within the Byzantine leadership who wanted a vigorous resistance; one was a warlike nobleman and political prisoner named Alexios Doukas, who was released and made the empire's *protovestiarios*. Robert de Clari also claimed that a 'Sultan of Konya' –

almost certainly Ghiyath al-Din Kaykhusraw I, who was currently a refugee in Constantinople – proposed an alliance with the Crusaders. The facts behind this story remain unknown, but, according to Robert, the Crusader leadership decided that, 'It would be dangerous to leave so great a thing as Constantinople in such case as it now was... When the sultan heard this he departed, sore displeased.' Ghiyath al-Din did indeed return to Anatolia, where the Saljuq civil wars continued.

The aged Isaac II was now almost certainly suffering from dementia. Meanwhile his son, Emperor Alexios IV, suggested a joint Crusader–Byzantine campaign to extend central-government control and hopefully capture the fugitive Alexios III. A Crusader force under Boniface of Montferrat, Henry of Flanders and Hugh of St Pol agreed to take part after being offered 'sixteen hundredweight of gold', according to Nicetas. So, in mid-August 1203, Alexios IV and his allies marched into Thrace, foraging widely and seizing several towns, including Adrianople, while Alexios III fled farther west.

Meanwhile, a riot broke out in Constantinople, during which Greeks killed a number of long-standing Latin residents, including Pisans and Amalfitans, who had previously supported the Byzantine Emperor. The survivors fled to join the Crusaders and Venetians, but the next day a band of armed Westerners retaliated, crossing the Golden Horn, attacking a small mosque that had been built as a token of friendship to Saladin, and started another fire, which burned until 21 August. It became one of the most extensive urban conflagrations in European history and rendered some 100,000 people homeless.

This time the people blamed Emperor Alexios IV for bringing the destructive Westerners to Constantinople. Arriving back in his capital, the young ruler tried to crush opposition by hanging all those involved in the deposing and blinding of his father, Isaac II, and seeming to distance himself from his hated allies. Nevertheless his popularity ebbed away, and, after a formal warning, Alexios IV stopped all further payments on 1 December

1203. For their part the Crusaders wanted what they believed the Emperor had promised them – namely the means to continue their crusade to the Holy Land. Therefore they ravaged and looted the surrounding territory to put pressure on the Byzantines.

This in turn resulted in skirmishing, in which, according to Nicetas, 'only Alexios Doukas… contriving to win the throne and the citizens' favour, dared to give battle against the Latins'. During one skirmish near Trypetos Lithos on 7 January his horse stumbled, and Alexios Doukas would have been captured 'had not a band of youthful archers from the City who happened to be present stoutly defended him'. Although the Byzantine leadership was divided about taking strong action against the Crusaders, considerable efforts went into strengthening the city's defences. Robert de Clari described how, during the winter of 1203–04, the Byzantines 'caused to be built atop these towers of stone goodly wooden towers. And these wooden towers did they overlay well on the outside with good planks and cover them over with good hides, so that they had no dread of the ladders or ships of the Venetians.'

The defenders also attempted to destroy the Venetian fleet moored within the Golden Horn. According to Robert de Clari, 'They seized the [Byzantine] ships within the city by night, and they caused them all to be filled with very dry wood, and pieces of swine's fat amongst the wood, then set they fire to them'. However, the Venetians were ready for these fireships and no damage was caused. The Byzantines tried the same tactic about a fortnight later, but again without success, 'save one merchant ship which was come there. This one was burned'. The Russian, Scandinavian or Varangian Guardsman whose recollections formed the basis of the *Novgorod Chronicle* maintained that 'Isokovic' (the son of Isaac II, namely Alexios IV) had warned the enemy.

On 25 January 1204 Byzantine patience finally snapped. There was rioting in the streets, and when Alexios IV turned to the Crusaders for support he was imprisoned by Alexios Doukas. Around the same time the aged and confused co-emperor Isaac II died. For a few days the mob also tried to force the Byzantine imperial crown upon a young nobleman called Nicholas Kanabos. The precise dating is unclear but Alexios Doukas now proclaimed himself Emperor and the unfortunate Nicholas Kanabos was executed. Alexios V Doukas was crowned on 5 February 1204, and for a while it looked as if the Byzantines had a determined ruler who could unite the capital against the Crusaders and Venetians. However, the Westerners still refused to abandon their protégée, who, being seen as a threat to the new Emperor, was strangled on the night of 7–8 February.

LEFT
The northern end of the landward walls of Constantinople, where they dip down to meet the walls along the Golden Horn. (Author's photograph)

RIGHT
The Story of St Nicaise, shown in a stained-glass window made shortly before or after the Fourth Crusade. (Louvre inv. OA 6006 and OA 6119, Paris. Author's photograph)

A stained-glass window in Canterbury Cathedral, made between 1190 and 1220. It illustrates a siege of the city by Danes and offers a vigorous image of the sort of combat faced by defenders and attackers during the Fourth Crusade. (Author's Photograph)

The scene was set for a final confrontation, and Alexios V continued to strengthen Constantinople's defences while conducting more-active operations outside the city. However, he desperately needed money, and so turned upon the many officials who had been raised to high rank by his predecessors, demanding large sums if they were to retain their positions.

In this crisis the Byzantine government also contacted the Saljuqs of Anatolia, but they were still involved in a civil war and could do nothing. Emperor Alexios V was on his own, though Crusader short-sightedness prevented his situation from being even worse. During the winter or early spring 1204 the Bulgarian leader, Ivan II, nicknamed 'Kaloyan the Roman Slayer', offered the Crusaders an alliance if they recognized Bulgarian independence. However, the Crusader leadership sent him a dismissive response, apparently regarding the Bulgarian leader as a rebel within territory they now wanted for themselves.

Around Constantinople, both sides now needed to forage for food. The Byzantines were not strong enough to stop the Crusaders from doing so, while the Crusader army was too small to prevent food convoys and additional Byzantine troops from entering the city. The biggest clash took place in February, when Emperor Alexios V led an ambush against Crusader foragers led by Henry of Hainault. The Crusaders were returning from the region of Phileas; though unidentified, it may have been what is now Kilyos on the Black Sea coast north of Constantinople.

Both sides were few in number, but when the Byzantines attacked the Crusaders adopted their standard defensive array, placing eight crossbowmen ahead of the mounted knights. Robert de Clari again provides the most dramatic account: 'The Emperor Mourtzouphlos [Alexios V] the traitor and the Greeks came toward them very swiftly and smote them fierce and fell; but, through God's mercy, never a one of the Franks did they unhorse. When the Franks saw the Greeks thus rushing upon them from every side, they let fall their lances and drew the coustiaus and misericordes [large and small daggers] that they had and began to defend themselves right hardily, and they slew many of them.'

The ambush force then fled, but some were overtaken: 'They let fall the Icon, and his imperial cloak, and the ensign with the Icon, which was all of gold and set with rich and precious stones.' This was a terrible loss for the Byzantines, as Nicetas explained: 'The icon of the Mother of God, which the Roman emperors reckon as their fellow general, was taken by the enemy.'

Alexios also tried to negotiate, but according to Nicetas the Venetians – whom he compares with 'wicked Telchines' (ancient sorcerers with webbed feet) – sabotaged Byzantine attempts to find a peaceful outcome. He also accused the Venetians of breaking a truce and trying to capture the Emperor when the latter met Doge Dandolo outside the Monastery of Sts Kosmas and Damian.

In March 1204 the Crusader and Venetian leadership decided on the outright conquest of Constantinople, and drew up a formal agreement to divide the Byzantine Empire between them. Any doubts that might have lingered amongst the rank and file were supposedly removed by the army's priests, who assured them than an attack upon Constantinople was morally equivalent to an assault on Muslim-held Jerusalem. Having learned valuable lessons from their previous attacks, the leadership focused on the Golden Horn fortifications, where the Venetians had previously been successful. So, during Lent, the attackers mounted stone-throwing siege weapons on many ships and scaling ladders on others. Nicetas claimed that, 'Banners were flown on top, and huge rewards were offered those who would ascend to give battle'. Nor were the Byzantine defenders idle, making the timber defences on top of their walls and towers even higher than before.

SECOND ASSAULT AND NEW EMPIRE

The Fourth Crusade's second assault on Constantinople started on 9 April 1204, but the previous day the men prepared to cross the Golden Horn. Villehardouin described how 'all entered into the vessels, and put their horses into the transports. Each division had its own ships, and all were ranged side by side, and the ships were separated from the galleys and transports.' He maintained that the front 'extended over full half a French league' or more than 1km, while Nicetas stated that the enemy assaulted the walls from the Blachernae Palace to the Monastery of Evergetes. Meanwhile, Emperor Alexios V established his command post next to the Pentapoptes Monastery, on a steep hill just inside the wall from which he could observe the enemy fleet, the Golden Horn and the threatened fortifications.

During medieval times part of the irregular southern shoreline of the Golden Horn lay at a distance from the fortifications, as it still does, but other stretches of shore were close enough for ships to approach very close to the defences. Consequently, some of the ships that crossed the Golden Horn early on 9 April 1204 disembarked their troops onto dry land; others came close enough to fight the defenders hand to hand.

Where there was sufficient space between walls and shore the Crusaders brought ashore 'armoured sheds' to protect their miners while Crusader crossbowmen shot at those on the fortifications who were in turn trying to drop missiles on the miners. The defenders also used incendiary weapons against the armoured sheds. It should be noted that during this period siege mining involved the excavation of shallow galleries, often lateral, to undermine the walls or towers. Furthermore, the Crusaders' miners were working at little more than a metre above sea level.

Unfortunately for the Crusaders, Byzantine counter-siege artillery proved notably effective, so that, in Robert de Clari's words, 'never a man durst remain within or beneath these [the Crusaders'] engines'. He also noted the fearsome effectiveness of the axe-armed English, Danes and Greeks who defended the walls. Elsewhere, the Venetians

The iron-covered wooden doors of the Balat Kapı ('Palace Gate'), which was probably the 'Imperial Gate' of Byzantine times, linking the Blachernae Palace to the Golden Horn. (Author's photograph)

KEY

Crusader movements ➡

Crusader encampments ▲

Byzantine movements ➡

Byzantine command positions ▲

BOUKOLEON PALACE

HIPPODROME

ST SOFIA CHURCH

AREA DESTROYED BY FIRE
19–20 AUGUST 1203

▼ EVENTS

1 8 April: Crusaders put their horses aboard the transport ships. Many Crusader and Venetian troops also go aboard late in the day.

2 8 April: Emperor Alexios V establishes his command post on the hill of the Pantepoptes Monastery.

3 9 April, early morning: Crusader and Venetian forces assault the Golden Horn fortifications, the Crusaders coming ashore where there is open ground between the fortifications and the shore. Some Venetian ships attack fortifications that are close enough to be assaulted directly from the ships' masts or yards.

4 9 April, evening: Around the time of vespers (evening prayer), the Doge of Venice summons a council of the Crusader leadership, probably in Galata.

5 10–11 April: Senior churchmen preach sermons to revive the Crusader army's morale while 'light women' are expelled from the camp.

6 12 April, dawn: Crusaders and Venetians attack same area.

7 12 April, afternoon: A strong northern wind drives ships farther ashore, enabling attackers to seize some towers and walls and to break through a blocked postern gate.

8 12 April, afternoon: Emperor Alexios V tries to counter-attack but then retreats to the Boukoleon Palace.

9 12 April, late afternoon: Crusaders and Venetians enter through four gates and capture the Emperor's hilltop command post. Boniface of Montferrat's troops are probably on the far left of the line.

10 Night of April 12–13: Alexios V flees westward.

11 Night of April 12–13: Byzantine fugitives disperse in many directions.

12 Night of April 12–13: Baldwin of Flanders establishes headquarters in Pantepoptes Monastery.

13 Night of April 12–13: The Byzantine leadership selects a new emperor, but he is unable to muster effective resistance.

14 Night of April 12–13: The Crusaders and Venetians ignite a third major fire.

15 13 April: Varangian Guard flees the city.

16 13 April: Boukoleon Palace surrenders to Boniface of Montferrat.

17 13 April: Blachernae Palace surrenders to Henry of Flanders.

18 13–15 April: The conquerors pillage, sack and slaughter for three days.

19 16 May: Count Baldwin of Flanders is crowned as first Latin Emperor of Constantinople.

THE SECOND SIEGE AND SACK OF CONSTANTINOPLE, 9–13 APRIL 1204

When the newly installed Byzantine Emperor Alexios was unable or unwilling to provide the Crusader army with the money it demanded, the Crusader leadership decided that the existing Byzantine government must be toppled.

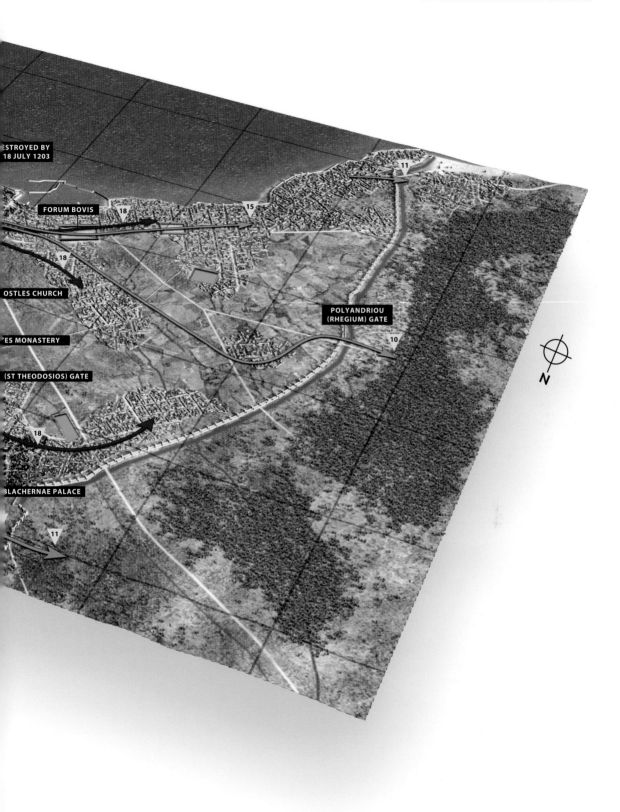

Note: Gridlines are shown at intervals of 1km/0.62miles

ESTROYED BY
18 JULY 1203

FORUM BOVIS

18

15

11

18

OSTLES CHURCH

18

POLYANDRIOU
(RHEGIUM) GATE

ES MONASTERY

10

(ST THEODOSIOS) GATE

18

BLACHERNAE PALACE

11

N

attempted to attack the walls directly from the rigging of their ships, but, furious as it was, this first assault failed, as Nicetas described: 'The Romans had the upper hand. Both the ships carrying the scaling ladders and the dromons transporting the horses were repulsed from the walls they had attacked without success, and many were killed by the stones thrown from the City's engines.' Villehardouin agreed: 'You must know that on that day those of the host lost more than the Greeks, and much were the Greeks rejoiced thereat.' The *Novgorod Chronicle* claims that 'the citizens killed about 100 Franks'.

As the dispirited attackers withdrew to the northern side of the Golden Horn, the Byzantines celebrated, as Robert de Clari witnessed: 'They began to hoot and to shout right lustily, and they went up upon the walls and let down their breeches and showed them their buttocks.' Having retreated back to their camp, the leaders of the Crusader and Venetian leaders held council in a church. Some now suggested they should attack Constantinople's southern seaward walls, but the Venetians pointed out that the current would carry their ships down the straits, so it was eventually agreed that another attack would be made on the Golden Horn walls on Monday.

Saturday and Sunday were spent repairing and refitting ships and siege weaponry. This time the vessels carrying scaling ladders would be lashed together in pairs, each of which would attack a single tower in order to outnumber the defenders. Robert de Clari described efforts to restore morale: 'Then did the bishops preach sermons throughout the host … and they showed the pilgrims that the battle was a righteous one, for that the Greeks were traitors and murderers, and that they were faithless… And an order was given that they should seek out and remove all the light women from the host, and send them very far away from the host.'

Early on Monday morning the Fourth Crusade launched another assault. This time, as Villehardouin noted: 'Those of the city stood in much less fear of them … and were in such good spirits that on the walls and towers you

Fully armoured knights attacking a tower with a battering ram, in the *Eneit*. (Ms. Germ. Fol. 282, f. 46v, Staatsbibliothek zu Berlin, Ms. Germ. Fol. 282, f. 46v, Berlin)

This singularly bloody combat scene shows knights in typical German arms and armour from the period of the Fourth Crusade. (*Jungfrauenspiegel*, Kestner Mus, Hannover)

could see nothing but people.' This time the Crusaders' siege bridges might have been longer, the *Novgorod Chronicle* maintaining that the attackers came in '40 great ships which had been tied to one another... Their other ships and galleys stayed back, fearing to be set afire.' In fact the horse-transports again beached in more open places, rather than attacking the fortifications directly.

Once again, the opposing armies bombarded each other with mangonels, crossbow bolts, arrows and incendiary weapons. The ships were of course vulnerable to fire, but so were the tall wooden structures that had been added to the tops of the city's stone towers. As Robert de Clari observed: 'The fire could not take hold there because of the hides wherewith the towers were covered. And those within the city ... were discharging some three score petraries [stone-throwing mangonels]... But the ships were so well covered with timber and with vine-cuttings that these did them no great mischief.'

The defenders prevailed until around midday, and Robert de Clari could see Emperor Alexios V directing on his hilltop command post, 'causing his trumpets to sound, and his timbrels, and making great display; and he was encouraging his men and ... sending them wheresoever he saw that the need was the greatest'.

Robert of Clari maintained that only four of five ships were tall enough to reach the tops of the Byzantine towers, and even when the attackers managed to reach these they seemed unable to get farther, even when the weather helped. Villehardouin described how the first tower was taken when a sudden northerly wind drove several ships farther ashore, including a linked pair named the *Pilgrim* and the *Paradise*, one being allocated to the Bishop of Soissons, which got so near a tower, 'the one on the one side and the other on the other ... that the ladder of the Pilgrim joined on to the tower'.

Robert de Clari described the same event, and how a Venetian and a Frenchman used the device that had been added as an assault ramp: 'And so soon as the ship hath fallen foul of this tower, the Venetian layeth hold with hands and feet, as best he can, and getting himself at last within the tower.'

PIERRE D'AMIENS AND ALEAUME DE CLARI BREAK INTO CONSTANTINOPLE, 12 APRIL 1204 (pp. 72–73)

As soon as men from one of the pairs of lashed-together Venetian assault ships managed to win control of the summit of a tower in the Golden Horn fortifications of Constantinople, ten knights and 60 other soldiers scrambled ashore on a narrow piece of ground between the water's edge and the neighbouring wall. Their leader had noticed a small but bricked-up postern gate, which his men immediately attacked with whatever instruments were available, including their own weapons. A hole big enough for a man was made, but the Crusaders were then daunted by the number of enemy waiting for them inside. At this point a clerk named Aleaume de Clari scrambled through despite his brother, the famous chronicler and knight Robert de Clari, grabbing him by the leg and trying

to pull him back. Aleaume was then joined by Pierre, the Châtelain of Amiens, who was an exceptionally tall, powerfully built and heavily armoured knight. The defenders, local militia rather than professional soldiers, were appalled by the sight of this huge Frenchman in his great helm 'shaped like a castle' and dared not attack him.

Just inside the fortification was the steep hill of the Pantepoptes Monastery, where the Byzantine Emperor Alexios V had established his command post. Seeing the danger posed by this Crusader breakthrough, the Emperor tried to launch a counter-attack, but his disheartened troops refused to close with the enemy. Constantinople was doomed.

The area just beyond the north-western fortifications of Constantinople is hilly and cut up by narrow valleys. It was here that the forces of the Fourth Crusade defeated the last major Byzantine sortie. (Author's photograph)

This courageous or foolhardy man was promptly attacked by the defenders, who 'cut him all in pieces' with axes and swords. But, as the waves pushed the ship forwards again, Andrew of Urboise (or Dureboise), 'lay hold with feet and hands to the tower until he gat himself up inside it, upon his knees'. Unlike his Venetian comrade, Andrew was fully armoured, so that the enemy's blows 'wounded him not', whereupon 'the knight rose up on his feet, and ... drew his sword'. This seemingly so frightened the defenders that the wooden upper tower was abandoned.

According to Nicetas the defenders were 'auxiliaries', meaning local militia rather than professional soldiers: 'The other knight came in after the first, and after him came in folk a plenty. And when they were within, they took strong ropes and stoutly lashed that ship to the tower, and when they had made her fast, there came in yet other folk a plenty.' However, the movement of the ship threatened to destroy the wooden tower, so it was cut adrift again.

Emperor Alexios V saw this threat and urged his troops to counter-attack, but, according to Robert de Clari, another ship made contact with a second tower, which was similarly taken. Even so, the Crusaders and Venetians held only the upper parts of these towers, not the walls on either side nor the ground beyond, where large numbers of defenders gathered. In this crisis Lord Peter, the *châtelain* of Amiens, led his 'ten knights and three score men-at-arms' to a small area of flat ground between the wall and shore where a postern gate had been bricked up.

The resulting break-in was described in detail by Robert de Clari, who took part along with his brother: 'And there was a certain clerk, Aleaume of Clari by name... Now when they were come to this postern gate they began to hack away at it right valiantly; but so thick flew the [crossbow] bolts and so many were the stones hurled down from the walls that it seemed in all likelihood they would be buried in the stones.' Other men had large shields, with which they protected those attacking the wall, but the Byzantine defenders also dropped pots of Greek fire. 'Yet did they hack away at that postern gate with axes and good swords, with timbers and bars and picks, until at last they made a great breach therein.' Beyond the passageway so many Byzantines were awaiting them that the Crusaders dared go no farther.

Robert's heroic brother now stepped forward: 'But when Aleaume the Clerk saw that none dare enter there, he sprang forward and said that he would go in. Now there was present a knight, his brother, Robert of Clari by name, who forbade him and said that he should by no means go in. And the clerk said that he would do so, and he gat himself in on his hands and feet.' Robert grabbed Aleaume's foot and tried to pull him back, 'but at last, despite his brother … the clerk went in. And when he was within, a multitude of the Greeks fell upon him, and they that were upon the walls began to cast down great stones at him. When the clerk saw this, he drew his knife and rushed upon them and made them to flee before him like cattle.' Then Aleaume de Clari shouted back, 'Sirs, enter boldly! For I see that they are utterly confounded and are fleeing away.'

Nicetas gives more credit to a particularly tall and heavily armoured French knight who should probably be identified as Peter of Amiens:

> A knight by the name of Peter entered through the gate situated there. He was deemed most capable of driving in rout all the battalions, for he was nearly nine fathoms tall [a poetic exaggeration taken from the ancient Greek Odyssey] and wore on his head a helmet fashioned in the shape of a towered city [a flat-topped great helm]. The noblemen about the emperor and the rest of the troops were unable to gaze upon the front of the helm of a single knight so terrible in form and spectacular in size and took to their customary flight as the efficacious medicine of salvation.

Robert de Clari pointed out that the knight was not really alone: 'My Lord Peter and his people came in. And there were not more than nine knights with him; nevertheless, there were some three score men at arms with him… And when they were within and they that were standing upon the walls in that place beheld them, then were these so greatly terrified that they … abandoned a great portion of the wall and fled.'

All the sources agree that Emperor Alexios V had the trumpets and drums sounded in an attempt to organize a counter-attack, though Robert de Clari dismissed this as merely a show of resistance: 'Then he made a great pretence of falling upon them and of spurring his horse, and he came about half-way up to them.' Lord Peter of Amiens encouraged his men, expecting a hard fight, but, 'When Mourtzouphlos the traitor saw that they would in no wise flee, he halted, and then he turned back to his tents.' The *Novgorod Chronicle* was shocked by the way the Emperor was abandoned by his followers: 'Emperor Mourtzouphlos was encouraging the boyars [noblemen] and all the people, wanting to fight … but they would not listen to him. They all ran away from him. The Emperor ran from them [the Franks], and they chased him to the Horse square [Hippodrome].'

Resistance now collapsed. Robert de Clari describes how Peter of Amiens' men went to the nearest gate and smashed it open from the inside, using axes and swords, 'until they broke the iron bolts, which were very strong, and the bars… And when the gate was opened and they that were without saw this, then they brought up their transports and led forth their horses and mounted them.' Villehardouin focused on the taking of four towers, after which, 'All begin to leap out of the ships and transports and galleys, helter-skelter, each as best he can, and they break in some three of the gates and enter in. And they draw the horses out of the transports; and the knights mount and ride straight to the quarters of Emperor Mourtzouphlos [Alexios V].'

This second siege of Constantinople, which resulted in the conquest of the Byzantine capital in 1204, hardly featured in Raimbaut de Vacqueyras' '*Epic Letter*', while other sources make no mention of Boniface of Montferrat, the nominal commander of the Fourth Crusade, nor of his troops. They must have been involved in the successful assault, but probably entered the city after the French and Venetians had broken in. The fact that Boniface also took control of the Boukoleon Palace, whereas Baldwin took the Blachernae Palace, suggests that the Marquis' men were at the western end, or left flank, of the attack. This might also account for Baldwin of Flanders rather than Boniface of Montferrat subsequently being chosen as the first Latin Emperor of Constantinople.

Robert de Clari noted that Emperor Alexios V abandoned his hilltop command post so quickly that 'his coffers and his jewels' were left behind, to be captured by Peter of Bracheux, while Nicetas reported that, having despoiled the Emperor's tents, the Crusaders took the Blachernae Palace without much resistance and established their own headquarters in the Pantepoptes Monastery, on the same hill that Alexios V had used as his command post. Meanwhile, as the Byzantine chronicler wrote: 'The emperor went hither and yon through the City's narrow streets, attempting to rally and mobilize the populace who wandered aimlessly about. Neither were they convinced by his exhortations nor did they yield to his blandishments.'

Eventually Alexios V gave up the struggle and returned to the Boukoleon Palace, which lay in the eastern part of the city, near St Sofia. During the night of 12–13 April he boarded a small ship along with Empress Euphrosyne, the wife of his predecessor Emperor Alexios III, and some of her daughters. According to the unsympathetic Nicetas, Alexios V passionately loved one of them, who was named Eudokia, 'for he had frequently engaged in sexual intercourse from the first appearance of hair on his cheek, and he was a proven lecher in bed, having put away two wedded wives'.

This early 13th-century wall painting of St Orestes comes from a church at Episkopi, which is now submerged beneath a reservoir. (Byzantine Museum, Athens)

The remaining Byzantine elite did not immediately surrender after Emperor Alexios V fled but instead tried to find a new emperor. Those who came forward as potential candidates were Constantine Doukas, who was probably the son of John Angelos Doukas and the uncle of Emperors Isaac II and Alexios III, and a certain 'Làskaris', who was probably either Constantine Laskaris or his brother Theodore Laskaris, who would become the future Emperor of Nicaea. Laskaris was chosen, but although he urged the army and people to resist, he found no real support, and, like most of the rest of the Byzantine aristocracy, soon had to flee the city. Nicetas was particularly disappointed by the way in which the elite Varangian Guard tried to use this crisis to extort higher wages. In the event they too had to flee the capital.

The following morning the Crusaders and Venetians found themselves, somewhat unexpectedly, in uncontested possession of Constantinople, Byzantine resistance having fizzled out during the night. Many of the city's wealthier citizens had by now fled, some pulling down the newly-built defences on the Golden Gate so that they could escape westwards towards Thrace and Macedonia – presumably accompanied by wagons loaded with their possessions. The 'holy warriors' of the Fourth Crusade now indulged in the worst orgy of massacre, pillage, rape and wanton destruction that the great city of Constantinople ever saw. The killing and devastation was far worse than the relatively restrained Ottoman conquest would be in 1453, and it brought the Fourth Crusade to a shocking end – at least in the Byzantine world.

THE FOURTH CRUSADE IN THE MIDDLE EAST

The actions of those elements of the Fourth Crusade that travelled the Middle East were militarily less successful than the conquest of Constantinople, though perhaps more honourable. Traditionally it was thought that very few members of this crusade reached the Holy Land in 1203, but that their actions nevertheless helped stabilize and even slightly extend the frontiers of the Kingdom of Jerusalem. More recent research suggests that over half those knights who took the cross in the Ile-de-France, but less than a tenth of those from Flanders, arrived in Acre. This would probably have amounted to a force of around 300 knights, plus a larger number of sergeants and other followers.

They found a somewhat confusing state of affairs. In fact the War of the Antioch Succession, having been in abeyance, had suddenly flared up late in 1202 when King Leo of Cilician Armenia reopened hostilities. This was followed by a serious Armenian raid into the fertile Jisr al-Hadid (Iron Bridge) area of the Principality of Antioch. Since then the local leadership had struggled to solve the question of the Antioch succession before the anticipated arrival of the main crusading army. These efforts involved the papal legate Soffred of Pisa sailing to Antioch, as well as Amaury the nominal King of Jerusalem, the Masters of both the Templars and the Hospitallers, local and

A carved relief showing the martyrdom of Sts Fuscien, Victoric and Gentian on their tomb in Sains-en-Amienois, with typical early 13th-century northern-French military equipment. (Author's photograph)

78

The view from the Crusader castle of Crac des Chevaliers across a fertile region that was often raided during the early 13th century. Beyond the hills lay the powerful Islamic city of Hims. (Author's photograph)

newly arrived barons including Stephen de Perche and Marcia of Hungary, plus an envoy sent by Boniface of Montferrat from outside Constantinople. But, despite their status, they nevertheless failed to achieve peace.

As if this was not frustrating enough for the enthusiastic Crusaders, the Kingdom of Jerusalem currently had a truce with its Ayyubid neighbours in Damascus and Egypt, so offensive action was not permitted on these fronts. There seems to have been no truce farther north, where the County of Tripoli and the Hospitaller garrison of Crac des Chevaliers were involved in low-intensity warfare with neighbouring Ayyubid garrisons. On 16 May 1203 this erupted into a major clash near Ba'rin (Montferrand) between Hospitallers and troops from Tripoli on one side and the Muslim garrison of Ba'albak on the other, with victory going to the Muslims. The Hospitaller castle of Montferrand itself had lost to Saladin at the end of the 12th century. There was another significant clash on 3 June, which the Muslims again won, though the Sultan of Hims remained in the field with his army, fearing another Christian attack.

According to the Arab chronicler Ibn Wasil, after this defeat the Hospitallers asked their Templar rivals to intercede on their behalf but the Ayyubid Sultan of Hims refused to make peace. The fact that those Crusaders who wanted to fight nevertheless did not get involved in this particular confrontation suggests that Count Bohemond IV, who ruled both Tripoli And Antioch, told them to back off. Frustrated, the Flemish leader Jean de Nesle went by sea to offer his services to King Leo of Cilicia, while Renard II of Dampierre, a high-ranking knight from Champagne, headed up the coast with the intention of offering his support to the garrison of Antioch.

The precise date of Renard's journey is unknown, though the renowned French historian Claude Cahen thought it was probably in May 1203, around the time of the battle at Ba'rin. It may, however, have been some months later, following angry arguments in Tripoli. More than 80 knights and a substantial number of infantry set out, perhaps to strengthen the position of the papal legate Soffred of Pisa rather than to take an active role in hostilities.

The Fourth Crusade in the Middle East

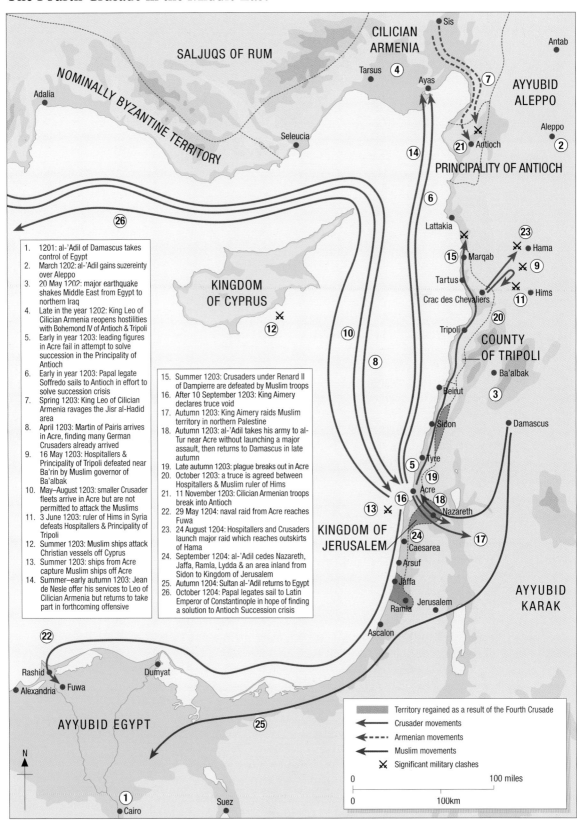

1. 1201: al-'Adil of Damascus takes control of Egypt
2. March 1202: al-'Adil gains suzereinty over Aleppo
3. 20 May 1202: major earthquake shakes Middle East from Egypt to northern Iraq
4. Late in the year 1202: King Leo of Cilician Armenia reopens hostilities with Bohemond IV of Antioch & Tripoli
5. Early in year 1203: leading figures in Acre fail in attempt to solve succession in the Principality of Antioch
6. Early in year 1203: Papal legate Soffredo sails to Antioch in effort to solve succession crisis
7. Spring 1203: King Leo of Cilician Armenia ravages the Jisr al-Hadid area
8. April 1203: Martin of Pairis arrives in Acre, finding many German Crusaders already arrived
9. 16 May 1203: Hospitallers & Principality of Tripoli defeated near Ba'rin by Muslim governor of Ba'albak
10. May–August 1203: smaller Crusader fleets arrive in Acre but are not permitted to attack the Muslims
11. 3 June 1203: ruler of Hims in Syria defeats Hospitallers & Principality of Tripoli
12. Summer 1203: Muslim ships attack Christian vessels off Cyprus
13. Summer 1203: ships from Acre capture Muslim ships off Acre
14. Summer–early autumn 1203: Jean de Nesle offer his services to Leo of Cilician Armenia but returns to take part in forthcoming offensive

15. Summer 1203: Crusaders under Renard II of Dampierre are defeated by Muslim troops
16. After 10 September 1203: King Aimery declares truce void
17. Autumn 1203: King Aimery raids Muslim territory in northern Palestine
18. Autumn 1203: al-'Adil takes his army to al-Tur near Acre without launching a major assault, then returns to Damascus in late autumn
19. Late autumn 1203: plague breaks out in Acre
20. October 1203: a truce is agreed between Hospitallers & Muslim ruler of Hims
21. 11 November 1203: Cilician Armenian troops break into Antioch
22. 29 May 1204: naval raid from Acre reaches Fuwa
23. 24 August 1204: Hospitallers and Crusaders launch major raid which reaches outskirts of Hama
24. September 1204: al-'Adil cedes Nazareth, Jaffa, Ramla, Lydda & an area inland from Sidon to Kingdom of Jerusalem
25. Autumn 1204: Sultan al-'Adil returns to Egypt
26. October 1204: Papal legates sail to Latin Emperor of Constantinople in hope of finding a solution to Antioch Succession crisis

Territory regained as a result of the Fourth Crusade
Crusader movements
Armenian movements
Muslim movements
Significant military clashes

0   100 miles

0   100km

Unfortunately Renard II of Dampierre ignored the advice of the governor of Jabal, the first Muslim town they reached along the coastal road, who had pointed out that the Ayyubid realms were currently in a state of some confusion, with truces sometimes being adhered to and sometimes not. The next town up the coast, Lattakia, was not apparently covered by any truce, so the governor of Jabal suggested that the travellers send messengers to Aleppo to get safe passage from Sultan al-Zahir of Aleppo, the overall ruler of the region. Unfortunately, the Crusaders considered they were strong enough to fight off any attack, and so pressed on. They were promptly ambushed by troops from Lattakia, several of the Christians being killed while others were captured, including Renard II of Dampierre.

Renard seems to have been held in Aleppo and freed late in 1203, apparently after the Hospitallers paid for most or all of his ransom. Jean de Villers and several other senior captives, including Godfrey of Guise and Bartholomew of Mézières, were probably held in Lattakia, perhaps being released later after military threats against this city by the nearby Hospitaller garrisons of Marqab and Crac des Chevaliers. They were certainly back in the Kingdom of Jerusalem by 1206, where their gifts to their local Hospitaller commanders were recorded. Two years later Godfrey of Guise is known to have been home in France.

The carvings around the western door of the Cathedral of St Lawrence in Trogir, on the Dalmatian coast, were made a few decades after the Fourth Crusade. (Author's photograph)

In October 1203, while these overconfident Crusaders were languishing in jail, a truce was at last agreed between the Hospitallers and the Sultan of Hims. However, the War of the Antioch Succession continued and on 11 November a small force of Cilician troops broke into Antioch, resulting in street fighting within the city. Another cause of dissension was the frontier castle of Baghras, which was claimed by both Cilician Armenia and the Principality of Antioch. Arguments about its possession still raged in July 1204. By then however, the truce between the Kingdom of Jerusalem and the Ayyubid Sultan al-'Adil had either come to an end or had broken down. In May 1204 a fleet of Crusader ships had sailed up the Rashid (Rosetta) branch of the river Nile, reaching deep into the Egyptian Delta to attack the little town of Fuwa. During that summer some Muslim ships retaliated, attacking Christian vessels off the coast of Cyprus, though apparently without authorization from al-'Adil. This prompted Christian galleys to seize six Muslim ships off the Palestinian coast.

A real war now seemed imminent, and some time after 10 September the Kingdom of Jerusalem declared that the truce with Damascus was also over. A substantial Christian force, almost certainly including members of the Fourth Crusade, attacked Muslim territory in Gallilee. Ibn al-Athir recorded these events but did not consider them very significant:

A large crowd of the Franks came out from overseas to Syria. Their mission was facilitated by their seizure of Constantinople... After their halt at Acre, they marched and looted several Muslim areas in the vicinity of (the river) Jordan... Al-Malik al-'Adil was in Damascus. He ordered his forces to muster in Syrian and Egyptian lands. He marched and camped at al-Tur near Acre... The Franks came out to meadows beyond Acre and raided Kafr Kanna near Nazareth. They took the inhabitants captive and confiscated their wealth. The amirs were urging al-'Adil to raid and plunder their domains, but he did not.

Clearly, al-'Adil still wanted to avoid a full-scale confrontation, or perhaps plague had already broken out in the crowded Crusader city. It certainly did so shortly afterwards, killing half of the newly arrived Crusader knights. Al-'Adil was also prepared to compromise, agreeing a renewed truce and even handing over a small (but significant) amount of land to the Kingdom of Jerusalem. These territories consisted of Nazareth and parts of the governorates of Ramla, Lydda and Sidon. Al-'Adil then returned to Egypt, which enabled the Crusaders to turn against the Muslim frontier city of Hama, which was not covered by the truce. Its ruler, al-Mansur, went out to face them in battle, probably in August 1204, but was badly beaten. After pursuing Sultan al-Mansur back to Hama, the Crusaders again defeated the city militia outside their walls.

Thus the Fourth Crusade came to an end in the Middle East as it already had in Constantinople. Even here its limited successes had been a result of Muslim weakness rather than Crusader strength. Al-'Adil was, in fact, currently in a difficult position. Several of his senior commanders were disloyal, his control over much of Syria was fragile and he still had not settled matters with the rival Muslim ruler of Mosul in northern Iraq. Probably fearing another larger Crusader attack on the Nile Delta following that of May 1204, he chose to seek peace on the best terms available. Furthermore, there was a famine in Egypt, compounding the Ayyubid ruler's shaky economic and financial position. Far to the south in Yemen, in the most distant of Ayyubid realms, the governors had been in trouble since 1201 and did not regain full control until 1214. Indeed, for the Muslims of the Middle East, the Fourth Crusade had been little more than a sideshow. For the Byzantines, of course, it had been a catastrophe.

AFTERMATH

The immediate aftermath of the Crusader conquest of Constantinople was mayhem. By the morning of 13 April the Byzantine aristocracy and ordinary citizens had either fled or ceased all resistance. During the night, however, the invaders were not sure of victory and so set further fires to extend the defensive perimeter already created by the previous year's fires. As before, the conflagration got out of control and, starting near the Monastery of Christ Evergetes, raged southwards 'to those areas that slope down to the sea and terminate in the vicinity of the Drungarios Gate,' as Nicetas recalled. This meant that the three fires caused by the Westerners had now destroyed about one-sixth of the area within the fortifications of Constantinople. Even Villehardouin was shocked, though he still underestimated the devastation: 'More houses had been burned in the city than there are houses in any three of the greatest cities in the kingdom of France.'

Most people tried to save themselves and their property, as Nicetas explained: 'The day waned and night came on, and each and every citizen busied himself with removing and burying his possessions. Some chose to leave the City, and whoever was able hastened to save himself.' There was no further resistance, and the following morning, when in some places the inhabitants lined the streets to welcome their new Emperor – whom they assumed would be the Marquis Boniface of Montferrat – the Crusaders and Venetians went on the rampage. As Villehardouin freely admitted: 'Then might you have seen the Greeks beaten down; and horses and palfreys captured, and mules, and other booty of killed and wounded there was neither end nor measure.'

The horrific sack of Constantinople by the Fourth Crusade in 1204 is perhaps reflected in this unusually expressive early 13th-century representation of the Massacre of the Innocents in the church of Norrey, Normandy. (Author's photograph)

In the 1960s many ships in the Golden Horn used a smoky fuel, while many houses were still heated by wood fires. Yet even this could not compare with the pall of devastation caused by the Fourth Crusade. (Author's photograph)

Boniface may well have believed that, as nominal leader of the Fourth Crusade, he would become the new ruler. He therefore rode along the eastern shore of Constantinople to the Boukoleon Palace of the Byzantine Emperors, which the officials ceremoniously handed over to him. Boniface thus took control of a huge amount of treasure as well as a 'larger number of the great ladies who had fled to the castle, for there were found the sister of the King of France, who had been empress, and the sister of the King of Hungary, who had also been empress, and other ladies very many'. Count Baldwin of Flanders' brother Henry similarly took control in Baldwin's name of the Blachernae Palace in the north-western corner of Constantinople. 'There too was found much treasure, not less than in the palace of Boukoleon,' Villehardouin recalled. 'Each garrisoned with his own people the castle that had been surrendered to him, and set a guard over the treasure.'

The scene seemed set for a civil war between the victors, but instead the victors' predatory energies were occupied in despoiling the city, which they did for three days without their leaders seriously attempting to stop them. According to Nicetas: 'The populace ... had turned out to greet them with crosses and venerable icons of Christ as was customary during festivals of solemn processions. But their disposition was not at all affected by what they saw... Instead, they plundered with impunity and stripped their victims shamelessly, beginning with their carts. Not only did they rob them of their substance but also the articles consecrated to God.' News of the sack spread across the Orthodox Christian world and beyond, to the Muslim world, where the Arab chronicler Abu Shama later noted: 'The Franks took possession of the kingdom, looted its treasures and all the fixtures and marbles of its churches. They then brought them to the lands of Egypt and Syria, where they were sold. Damascus has seen plenty of that marble.' In fact, this sale of valuable stone probably took place later, when the new Latin Empire of Constantinople was desperate for money. Most of the booty went westwards, to Europe and in particular to Venice, where for centuries four huge gilded bronze horses stood on the façade of the Basilica of San Marco as a constant reminder of the Fourth Crusade.[11]

11 The orginals were transferred to the San Marco Museum, inside the church, during the 1990s and were replaced by replicas.

The Latin Empire at its greatest extent

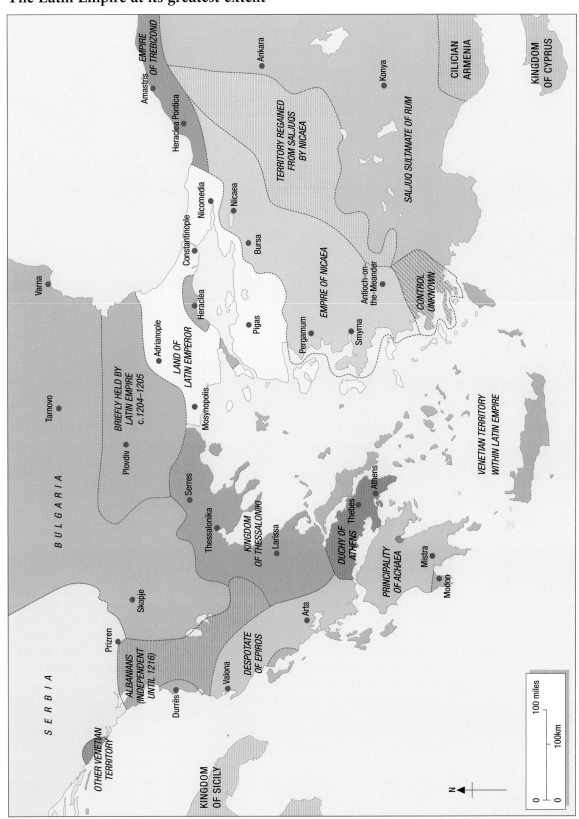

EMPIRE OF TREBIZOND

Ankara

Amastris

Heraclea Pontica

KINGDOM OF CYPRUS

CILICIAN ARMENIA

Konya

TERRITORY REGAINED FROM SALJUQS BY NICAEA

SALJUQ SULTANATE OF RUM

Nicomedia

Nicaea

Constantinople

Bursa

Varna

Heraclea

Adrianople

LAND OF LATIN EMPEROR

Pigas

Pergamum

EMPIRE OF NICAEA

Antioch-on-the-Meander

Smyrna

CONTROL UNKNOWN

BRIEFLY HELD BY LATIN EMPIRE c.1204–1205

Tarnovo

Mosynopolis

Plovdiv

VENETIAN TERRITORY WITHIN LATIN EMPIRE

Serres

B U L G A R I A

Thessalonika

KINGDOM OF THESSALONIKI

Larissa

Athens

Thebes

DUCHY OF ATHENS

Skopje

Mistra

PRINCIPALITY OF ACHAEA

Prizren

Arta

Modon

ALBANIANS (INDEPENDENT UNTIL 1216)

DESPOTATE OF EPIROS

S E R B I A

Valona

Durrës

OTHER VENETIAN TERRITORY

KINGDOM OF SICILY

100 miles

100km

N

0

0

85

During the second week of May, to Boniface of Montferrat's surprise and anger, Baldwin of Flanders was chosen as the first ruler of a newly established 'Latin Empire of Constantinople', being crowned on the 16th. Baldwin had clearly played a more active front-line role during the sieges of 1203 and 1204, yet his rule would be brief, and the Latin Empire itself lasted only until 1261. Nevertheless, tensions between Baldwin and Boniface almost led to violence. The loyal Raimbaut de Vacqueyras seems to have served as the disappointed Marquis of Montferrat's mouthpiece, writing a poem a month or so later in which he accused the new Emperor of sloth in the face of enemies as well as a lack of generosity towards his comrades. Raimbaut's call for Baldwin to continue the original purpose of the crusade by going to the aid of the Kingdom of Jerusalem may also have reflected divided opinion within the Crusader army:

> And let him not fear cold or heat,
> Nor linger in palatial ease, for he has placed on his neck a burden
> Of such weight that, if he be not of great valour,
> It will be hard for him to bear it to the end.
> For the Wallachians and the Cumans and the Russians
> And the Turks and the Pagans and the Persians
> Will be against him, with the Greeks.
> And if he does not endure toil for glory's sake,
> He may undo all he has done.[12]

Raimbault's prediction of the multiple enemies and problems that the newly created Latin Empire would face proved prophetic.

The Crusader clergy had convinced the rank and file that their attack on Christian Constantinople was consistent with their original crusading vow, and Cardinal Peter Capuano now confirmed that defence of the city for a further year would complete that vow. He and his colleague, Cardinal Soffredo, also lifted the excommunication of the Venetians, even though they still refused to admit they had been wrong to attack Zadar back in 1202.

---

12 Fourth verse of 'Sirventes XX', in J. Linskill, *The Poems of The Troubadour Rainbault de Vaqueiras* (The Hague, 1964) p. 228.

TOP
The largest territory acquired by Venice in the aftermath of the Fourth Crusade was the island of Crete, though only to prevent its falling to the Venetians' great rivals, the Genoese. (Author's photograph)

BOTTOM
The Lefke Gate of Nicaea (Iznik), where the most powerful of the fragmented Byzantine successor states was established after the Fourth Crusade. (Author's photograph)

While these internal problems were gradually overcome, relations between the newly established Latin Empire and Bulgaria were worsening fast. Later in 1204 Tsar Kaloyan even sent a letter to the pope in Rome, warning that the situation could lead to conflict: 'Write to the Latins, to keep them from my empire, and, if they do, my empire will not harm them, but let them not set it at little worth. If they make an attempt against my empire ... and some of them get killed, do not your Holiness suspect my empire because it will not be my fault.'[13]

As it happened, the Latin Empire set all its new neighbours 'at little worth' and attempted to take over what had been claimed as Byzantine territory at the end of the 12th century. In many areas the Latins were successful, creating a Kingdom of Thessaloniki, which was allocated to Boniface of Montferrat,

---

13 Wolff, R. L., 'The 'Second Bulgarian Empire', Its Origins and History to 1204' in *Speculum*, 24 (1949) p. 198.

LEFT
Following the conquest of Constantinople, the Venetians were not interested in extensive territory, but instead demanded various coasts and strategic ports such as Heraclea (Marmara Ereğlisi). (Author's photograph)

RIGHT
Another Byzantine successor state that emerged from the wreckage of the Fourth Crusade was the Empire of Trebizond (Trabzon) on the Black Sea coast of Anatolia. (Author's photograph)

a Duchy of Athens and a Principality of Achaea, which were theoretically subject to Thessaloniki. The Latin Empire itself briefly occupied part of north-western Anatolia, but then sought to extend its authority in parts of Thrace also claimed by Bulgaria. The result was a disastrous defeat outside Adrianople (Edirne) in April 1205 in which Emperor Baldwin was captured and taken to the Bulgarian capital of Tarnovo where he later died. Louis of Blois, Latin claimant to most of the Byzantine territories in Anatolia, was also killed. Baldwin's brother Henry took over as the second Latin Emperor, ruling with some success until 1216. On 4 September 1207, however, the Bulgarians also defeated and killed Boniface of Montferrat, King of Thessaloniki, near the little Thracian town of Mosynopolis, which thereafter remained abandoned. The only Western power to enjoy long-term benefit from the Fourth Crusade was Venice. In addition to his share of the vast booty from Constantinople, Doge Dandolo had been very selective in his country's share of the conquered territory. Although some of these new gains were held for only a few decades, others would remain in Venetian hands until the early 18th century.

Meanwhile the initially demoralized Byzantines soon re-established three significant, but frequently competing, successor states: the Empire of Nicaea (Iznik) under a Laskarid dynasty, the Empire of Trebizond (Trabzon) under a Comnenid dynasty and the so-called Despotate of Epiros, whose dynasty sprang from the Doukas family, which never actually claimed the traditional Byzantine title of 'despot'. It is often said that the Fourth Crusade broke Byzantine power and thus opened up south-eastern Christendom to Ottoman Turkish conquest. In fact the establishment of a strong Byzantine successor 'empire' based upon the fortified city of Nicaea actually pushed back the Turkish frontier for nigh on half a century. It was only when a new Emperor of Nicaea, Michael VIII Palaiologos, regained Constantinople in 1261 that Byzantine interest in its Anatolian frontier again declined, eventually making possible the staggering Ottoman conquests of the 14th century.

THE BATTLEFIELD TODAY

The Fourth Crusade is unusual because, despite having extended over a very considerable distance, virtually all the places involved are in what might be considered mainstream tourist areas. Even areas where the preaching of a new crusade was most vigorous, and from which the largest number of participants or their leaders came, are often visited for entirely different reasons. This is true of the Champagne and Artois regions of France, the historic cities of Belgian Flanders, the Piedmont area around Montferrat in north-western Italy and, more obviously, the fabulous city of Venice. All these areas have abundant hotel accommodation in all classes, as well as an astonishing variety of historical buildings surviving from before, or around the time of, the Fourth Crusade.

The campaign itself was a naval expedition with three major sieges. Unfortunately, the majority of us who enjoy tracing medieval campaigns do not have private yachts. For those that do, the author suggests that this would be the voyage of a lifetime! For the rest of us, the best way to travel 'in the wake' of the crusade is by car along the nearby coasts. The Crusaders themselves camped for months on the Lido, just across the lagoon from Venice. This has a large number of excellent campsites, while the problem of summer mosquitoes has largely been solved. Travelling along the northern

The members of the Fourth Crusade were astonished by the massive Hagia Sophia in Constantinople. The minarets date from after the Ottoman conquest. (Fred Nicolle photo)

and eastern coasts of the Adriatic is necessarily slow, but offers some of the most beautiful scenery in Europe. The route also passes picturesque beautiful and historic coastal towns. Zadar is not one of the most scenic but it can boast interesting early modern fortifications as well as a number of magnificent medieval buildings, including two churches from before the Fourth Crusade. Furthermore, the short coast of Slovenia and the longer Dalmatian coast of Croatia have abundant hotels and other tourist facilities.

The Crusaders paused for some time on Corfu, which is of course a major tourist destination. Their next significant landfalls were on the large island of Evvoia and the neighbouring smaller island of Andros, both of which have all necessary facilities, not to mention harbours for our fortunate yachtsmen. The most important events of the Fourth Crusade nevertheless took place in Turkey. Once again these were within the touristically developed north-western part of the country, being centred upon the magnificent city of Istanbul (Constantinople). Before reaching that destination, however, the Crusader fleet stopped at Abydos, which is one of very few places on this voyage that is partly inaccessible to visitors because the town of Abydos, known as Mysia in ancient times and now called Naru Burnu, was located on the promontory and harbour of Nara Burnu, part of which remains a closed military zone.

The invaders then sailed to Chalcedon (now Kadıköy), which is now one of the suburbs of Istanbul lying on the Anatolian shores of the Bosporus, before going slightly farther north to Skoutarion (now Üsküdar). Both of these Asiatic suburbs have a variety of hotels in all price ranges, some excellent restaurants and bustling traditional Turkish markets. They are also connected to the old city of Istanbul by frequent ferry services, which make this Anatolian suburb a good centre from which to visit the city. Furthermore, there are reasonably priced long-term parking facilities in Üsküdar.

Militarily, the Fourth Crusade focused upon three distant parts of Istanbul: Galata, the fortifications along the Golden Horn and the Blachernae Palace. Virtually nothing remains from the middle Byzantine period in Galata, since the great tower now known as the Galata Tower is a late-medieval structure located on the top of the hill rather than down at the water's edge like the tower attacked by the Fourth Crusade. The beach where the Crusaders came ashore has also changed out of all recognition, having been consolidated into a series of quays. Amongst them are terminals for some of the many ferry routes that operate up and down the Bosporus.

In contrast, the medieval Byzantine fortifications along the Golden Horn shore of Istanbul are remarkably well preserved, especially towards their western end. In many places walls, towers and even gates still have later structures such as houses and workshops attached to their inner faces and upper parts. The narrow open ground between these fortifications and the waters of the Golden Horn has, however, been cleared and extended so that it is difficult to imagine the superstructures of Venetian ships getting entangled with the towers, or even to see the Crusaders bringing their horses ashore under heavy fire from Byzantine defenders.

The Blachernae Palace area, where the Golden Horn fortifications meet the more famous landward walls of Constantinople, is easy to observe and understand, despite the network of modern main roads which apparently cover the place where the main Crusader encampment and siege works lay. To the west the land still looks wooded and green, though this is an illusion created by the trees, which partially obscure suburbs farther west. The latter include Eyüp, which covers what was the Monastery of Sts Kosmas and Damian. Inside the massive 12th-century fortifications of the Blachernae area the Palace of Porphyrogenitos (Tekfur Sarayı) is the main surviving element of the palatial complex.

FURTHER READING

Andrea, A., *Contemporary Sources for the Fourth Crusade* (Leiden, 2000)

Angold, M. J., 'The Road to 1204: the Byzantine background to the Fourth Crusade', *Journal of Medieval History*, 25 (1999) pp. 257–78

——, *The Byzantine Empire 1025–1204* (London, 1984)

——, *The Fourth Crusade: event and context* (London, 2003)

Arbel, B., and Hamilton, B. (eds.), *Latins and Greeks in the Eastern Mediterranean after 1204* (London, 1989)

Azhari, T. El-, 'Muslim Chroniclers and the Fourth Crusades', *Crusades*, 6 (2007) pp. 107–16

Banescu, N., *Un probleme d'histoire medievale. Création et caractère du second empire bulgare* (Bucharest, 1942)

Bartusis, M. C., *The Late Byzantine Army: Arms and Society 1204–1453* (Philadelphia, 1992)

Bell, G. D., 'Unintended Consumption: The Interruption of the Fourth Crusade', *Journal of Medieval Military History*, 6 (2008) pp. 79–94

Blondal, S., and Benediktz, B. S., *The Varangians of Byzantium* (Cambridge, 1978)

Bonenfant, P., 'La Noblesse en Brabant aux XIIe et XIIIe siècles', *Le Moyen Age*, 64 (1958) pp. 27–66

Brand, C. M., *Byzantium Confronts the West: 1180–1204* (Cambridge, MA, 1968)

Brunelli, Vitaliano, *Storia della città di Zara : Dai tempi più remoti sino al 1409* (Trieste, 1974)

Cessi, R., 'Venice on the Eve of the Fourth Crusade', in J. M. Hussey (ed.), *Cambridge Medieval History, vol. 4* (Cambridge, 1966) pp. 251–74

Cole, P. J., *The Preaching of the Crusades to the Holy Land 1095–1270* (Cambridge, MA, 1991)

Crouzet-Pavan, E., 'Quand le doge part à la croisade...' in J. Paviot and J. Verger (eds.), *Guerre, pouvoir et noblesse au Moyen Age* (Paris, 2000) pp. 167–74

Dawkins, R. M., 'The Later History of the Varangian Guard, some notes', *Journal of Roman Studies*, 37 (1947) pp. 39–46

Dufournet, J., *Villehardouin et Clari* (Paris, 1973)

Ferluga, 'L'aristocratie byzantine en Morée au temps de la conquête latine', *Byzantinische Forschungen*, 4 (1972) pp. 76–87

Ferrard, C. G., 'The Amount of Constantinopolitan Booty in 1204', *Studi Veneziani*, 13 (1971) pp. 95–104

Foss, C., and Winfield, D., *Byzantine Fortifications: an Introduction* (Pretoria, 1986)

Fotheringham, J. K., 'Genoa and the Fourth Crusade', *English Historical Review*, 25 (1910) pp. 26–57

Frances, E., 'Sur la conquête de Constantinople par les Latins', *Byzantinoslavica*, 15 (1934) pp. 21–26

Frolow, A., *Recherches sur la Déviation de la IVe Croisade vers Constantinople* (Paris, 1955)

Godfrey, J., *1204: The Unholy Crusade* (Oxford, 1980)

——, 'The Novgorod Account of the Fourth Crusade', *Byzantion*, 43 (1973) pp. 297–311

Gunther of Pairis (A. Andrea, ed.), *The Capture of Constantinople: The Hysteria Constantinopolitana of Gunther of Pairis* (Philadelphia, 1996)

Halphen, L., 'Le rôle des Latins dans l'histoire intérieure de Constantinople à la fin du XIIe siècle', in anon. (ed.), *Mélanges Charles Diehl, I* (1930) pp. 141–45

Harris, J., 'Collusion with the infidel as a pretext for military action against Byzantium', in S. Lambert and E. James (eds.), *Clash of Cultures: the Languages of Love and Hate* (Turnhout, 2010)

——, 'The Problem of Supply and the Sack of Constantinople', in P. Piatti (ed.), *The Fourth Crusade Revisited* (Vatican City, 2008) pp. 145–54

Hendrickx, B., 'A propos du nombre des troupes de la quatrième croisade et de l'empereur Baudoin I', *Byzantina*, 3 (1971) pp. 29–41

——, 'Les Arméniens d'Asie Mineure et de Thrace au début de l'Empire Latin de Constantinople', *Revue des Etudes Arméniennes*, 22 (1991) pp. 217–23

——, 'Les institutions de l'Empire Latin de Constantinople (1204–1261): le pouvoir imperial', *Byzantina*, 6 (1974) pp. 85–154

Hendy, M. F., 'Byzantium, 1081–1204: An Economic Reappraisal', *Transactions of the Royal Historical Society*, 5 ser. 20 (1970) pp. 31–52

Herrin, J., 'The Collapse of the Byzantine Empire in the Twelfth Century', *University of Birmingham Historical Journal*, 12 (1969–70) pp. 188–203

Jacoby, D., 'Byzantium, the Italian Maritime Powers and the Black Sea before 1204', *Byzantinische Zeitschrift*, 100 (2007) pp. 677–99

——, 'Italian Privileges and Trade in Byzantium before the Fourth Crusade; A Reconsideration', *Anuario de estudios medievales*, 24 (1994) pp. 349–69

Karlin-Hayter, P., 'Notes sur le LATINIKON dans l'armée et les historiens de Nicée', *Byzantinische Forschungen*, 4 (1972) pp. 142–50

Kazhdan, A., 'Terminology of Warfare in the History of Niketus Choniates: Contingents and Battle', in K. Tsiknakis (ed.), *Byzantium at War (9th–12th c.)* (Athens, 1997) pp. 75–91

Kedar, B. Z., 'The Fourth Crusade's Second Front', in A. Laiou (ed.), *Urbs Capta: The Fourth Crusade and its Consequences* (Paris, 2005) pp. 89–110

Lilie, R-J., (tr. J. C. Morris and J. E. Ridings), *Byzantium and the Crusader states 1096–1204* (Oxford, 1993)

Linskill, J., *The Poems of the Troubadour Raimbault de Vaqueiras* (The Hague, 1964)

Lock, P., *The Franks in the Aegean, 1204–1500* (London, 1995)

Longnon, J., *Les compagnons de Villehardouin: recherches sur les croisés de la quatrième croisade* (Paris, 1978)

Longnon, L., 'Les troubadours à la cour de Boniface de Monferrat en Italie et en Orient', *Revue et synthese*, ns. 23 (1948) pp. 45–60

Lurier, H. E. (tr.), *Crusaders as Conquerors: The Chronicle of the Morea* (New York, 1964)

——, 'The Fires of the Fourth Crusade in Constantinople, 1203–1204; A Damage Assessment', *Byzantinische Zeitschrift*, 84/85 (1992) pp. 72–93

——, *Enrico Dandalo and the rise of Venice* (Baltimore, 2003)

Madden, T., and D. Queller, *The Fourth Crusade* (Phildelphia, 1996)

Marzials, F., (tr.), *Memoirs of the crusades by Villehardouin and de Joinville* (London, 1921)

Meschini, M., 'The '4 Crusades' of 1204', in T. Madden (ed.), *The Fourth Crusade: Event, Aftermath, Perceptions* (Aldershot, 2008) pp. 27–42

Moravcsik, J., 'Les Relations entre la Hongrie et Byzance à l'epoques des Croisades', *Revue des Etudes Hongroises*, 8–9 (1933) pp. 301–08

Morris, C., 'Villehardouin and the Conquest of Constantinople', *History*, 53 (1968) pp. 24–34

Nasturel, P. S., 'Valaques, Coumans et Byzantines sous la règne de Manuel Comnène', *Byzantina*, 1 (Thessalonika, 1969)

Nicetas Choniates (H.J. Magoulias tr.), *O City of Byzantium, Annals of Nicetas Choniates* (Detroit, 1984)

Nicol, D.M., *Byzantium and Venice: A Study in Diplomatic and Cultural Relations* (Cambridge, 1988)

Noble, P. S., '1204, The Crusade Without Epic Heroes', in P. E. Bennett (et al. eds.), *Epic and Crusade* (Edinburgh, 2006) pp. 89–104

——, 'Eyewitnesses of the Fourth Crusade; the reign of Alexios V', in E. Kooper (ed.), *The Medieval Chronicle, II* (New York, 2002) pp. 178–89

——, 'Eyewitnesses to the Fourth Crusade – the war against Alexios III', *Reading Medieval Studies*, 25 (1999) pp. 75–89

Ostrogorsky, G., 'Les Coumans proniaires', *Annuaire de l'Institut de Philologie et d'Histoire orientales et Slaves*, 11 (1951)

Phillips, J. P., *The Fourth Crusade and the Sack of Constantinople* (London, 2005)

Pokorny, R., 'Zwei Unedierte Briefe aus der Frühzeit des Lateinischen Kaiserreichs von Konstantinople', *Byzantion*, 55 (1985) pp. 180–209

Primov, B., 'The papacy, the Fourth Crusade and Bulgaria', *Byzantino-Bulgarica*, 1 (1962) pp. 183–211

Pryor, J. H., 'The Chain of the Golden Horn, 5–7 July 1203', in I. Shagrir (et al. eds.), *In Lauden Hierosolymitani; Studies in Crusades and Medieval Culture in Honour of Benjamin Z. Kedar* (Aldershot, 2007) pp. 369–84

——, 'The Venetian Fleet for the Fourth Crusade and the Diversion of the crusade to Constantinople', in N. Housley and M. Bull (eds.), *The Experience of Crusading, vol. 1: Western Approaches* (Cambridge, 2003) pp. 103–23

Queller, D. E., and T. F. Madden, *The Fourth Crusade: the conquest of Constantinople 1201–1204* (second revised edition, Philadelphia, 1997)

Riley-Smith, J., 'The Hospitaller Commandery of Eterpigny and a Postscript of the Fourth Crusade in Syria', in I. Shagrir (et al. eds.), *In Lauden Hierosolymitani* (Aldershot, 2007) pp. 385–93

Robert de Clari (E. H. McNeal tr.), *The Conquest of Constantinople* (London, 1936)

Robert de Clari (P. Noble ed.), *La Conquête de Constantinople: Société Rencesvals British Branch, British Rencesvals Publications 3* (Edinburgh, 2005)

Robert de Clari, 'La Conquête de Constantinople', in A. Pauphilet and E. Pognon (eds.), *Historiens et chroniqueurs du Moyen Age* (Paris, 1952)

Savvides, A. G. C., 'Sulayman Shah of Rum, Byzantium, Cilician Armenia and Georgia, AD 1197–1204', *Byzantion*, 73 (2003) pp. 96–111

——, 'The Kleinchronikon on Byzantium's Relations with the Seljuks and on the Oriental Frankish Kingdom's Relations with Saladin and the Mamelukes (AD: 1067–1291)', *Journal of Oriental and African Studies*, 1 (1989)

Siberry, E., *Criticism of Crusading 1095–1274* (Oxford, 1985)

Sweeney, J. R., 'Hungary and the crusades, 1169–1218', *International History Review*, 3 (1981) pp. 467–81

Vasary, I., *Cumans and Tatars: oriental military in the pre-Ottoman Balkans 1185–1365* (Cambridge, 2005)

Villehardouin, 'La Conquête de Constantinople', in A. Pauphilet and E. Pognon (eds.), *Historiens et chroniqueurs du Moyen Age* (Paris, 1952)

Villehardouin, Geoffrey de (C. Smith tr.), *Chronicles of the crusades* (London, 2008)

Villehardouin, Geoffrey de (J. Dufournet ed. and tr.), *Geoffrey de Villehardouin: La Conquete de Constantinople* (Paris, 1973)

Wolff, R. L., 'Baldwin of Flanders and Hainaut, First Latin Emperor of Constantinople; His Life, Death, and Resurrection, 1172–1225', *Speculum*, 27 (1952) pp. 281–322

——, 'The 'Second Bulgarian Empire', Its Origins and History to 1204', *Speculum*, 24 (1949) pp. 167–206

INDEX

References to illustrations are shown in **bold**.
Plates are shown with page in **bold** and caption in brackets, e.g. **4** (5).